WINGING IT!

Winging it!

THE ADVENTURES OF TIM WALLIS

NEVILLE PEAT

Longacre Press

Photography credits: all photographs are from the
Alpine Deer Group collection unless otherwise acknowledged.

Winging It! The Adventures of Tim Wallis is based on the biography
Hurricane Tim: The Story of Sir Tim Wallis, also by Neville Peat.

ISBN 978 1 877361 50 0

First published by Longacre Press, 2006
30 Moray Place, Dunedin, New Zealand
www.longacre.co.nz

Reprinted 2007

A catalogue record for this book is available
from the National Library of New Zealand.

Book and cover design by Christine Buess
Front cover photo: Tim Wallis flying his Spitfire Mk XVI over Wanaka. Phil Makanna
Map on page 17 from *Pick of the Bunch: New Zealand Wildflowers*
by Peter Johnson, Longacre Press, 1997
Map on page 78 reproduced with permission
from Lonely Planet Publications ©2006
Printed by Astra Print, Wellington, New Zealand

CONTENTS

Tim Wallis with a stag he shot in 1960 up the Okuru Valley, South Westland.

WHIRLWIND ADVENTURE

TAKE A WILD ANIMAL (red deer) in plague numbers, spread them across a remote and rugged terrain (Fiordland and the Southern Alps), throw in helicopters hell-bent on shooting or recovering them live, then add a daring pilot called Tim Wallis – these are the ingredients of a whirlwind adventure story.

This is Tim's story. It's about the way he built a career and a multi-million-dollar business out of a weekend hobby, deerstalking. It's about how he used helicopters where they'd never been before, and about exploring new frontiers in New Zealand and other parts of the world. Tim – Sir Tim at formal occasions – is a pioneer of deer farming in New Zealand, and that passion has taken him from Canada to Vanuatu and even Siberia.

Since the mid-1980s he has ventured into tourism and vintage warplanes. He's collected Second World War fighter aircraft from around the world and every two years you can see them in action at Warbirds Over Wanaka, an event he founded in 1988.

Tim's had quite a few accidents over the years. When he was 29 his helicopter hit power lines and crashed and he was told he might not walk again. But he did. In 1996 he crashed a Spitfire upside down and suffered shocking head injuries. This time the doctors said he might not live. But he did. Tim's a survivor. So in addition to the adventure and the drama, this is also a story about how Tim has beaten the odds with his never-say-die attitude.

He has a rare kind of fighting spirit. In a country where heroes are mostly found in sport, he's legendary.

I chose the year 1968 as a starting point for the story. It's a terrific year in his life. In 1968 he caught red deer live for experimental farming, he used ships in Fiordland for processing the venison, and he met Prue Hazledine, who would become his wife a few years later. It was also the year he broke his back and faced business failure. How did he survive? Read on and be inspired.

Neville Peat
Broad Bay, Otago Peninsula
February 2006

Tim refuelling a Hiller 12E helicopter in the East Matukituki Valley in 1967. Robert Wilson

CHAPTER 1

DARING AND DETERMINED

THE DAY TIM WALLIS broke his back, the lights went out in Queenstown. Across the whole area, in homes, hotels, shops and cafes, the power was off for three hours amidst the coldest weather in 40 years. Up on the slopes of Coronet Peak, the chairlift stopped suddenly, leaving skiers swinging in mid-air till the emergency generator got going. What had happened?

Tim Wallis had crashed.

Tim had been carting hay by helicopter to sheep stranded and starving in deep snow near Queenstown. It was a beautifully fine day, blue above, white below – a great day for skiing. Tim spent a chilly morning feeding out the stock and carrying farm hands to the high ground so they could tramp escape routes for the sheep through the snow. In the afternoon he intended to pick up his girlfriend Prue in the helicopter and go with friends to Coronet Peak. He liked mixing business and pleasure. To Tim, business meant busyness. He thrived on it. His booming business now ran a fleet of four helicopters, two ships and a factory that processed venison from red deer shot in the southern mountains of New Zealand.

That Sunday morning in July 1968, with the Queenstown job completed, he flew off towards Frankton, a different direction. He had two passengers with him. None of them saw the high-voltage power lines strung across a gap between the hills. The lines carried the main power supply for Queenstown and surrounding areas.

Suddenly, the air overhead seemed to explode as the main rotor blades chopped through the lines. At that

Tim Wallis in a Hiller helicopter at Makarora, 1967. Dave Osmers

moment, you might think the helicopter would plummet to the ground. But it didn't. For a few agonising moments, with its engine screaming, it continued upwards as the steel power lines strangled the rotor control rods and increased the pitch on the blades. Then the helicopter dropped like a rock.

A helicopter can fly for a short time without power and may land undamaged so long as the pilot can direct the rotor blades. But with the blades bound up and the machine unable to glide, there was no chance of a soft landing.

The Hiller fell more than 50 metres. It crashed onto a flat paddock covered by ankle-deep snow, lurching to the right on impact. In the middle seat of the three-seater machine, Tim knew he was badly injured. He had no feeling at all below his waist. He couldn't move. The men on either side of him were also seriously injured but one of them managed to walk to a nearby farmhouse and

Wreckage of the Hiller 12E, ZK-HBF, that struck power lines at Queenstown Hill station. The helicopter is lying on its side with the remains of the instrument panels protruding.

raise the alarm. An ambulance turned up, reaching the crash site towed by a farmer's tractor.

The injuries to Tim and his passengers were too severe for Queenstown's hospital to treat so they drove on to the larger Invercargill Hospital, over two hours south. Three days later Tim was flown to Christchurch Hospital's spinal injury unit for more specialised treatment. Low down on his spine, two vertebrae – the ones most vulnerable to vertical impact – were crushed. To aid healing and any chance of his walking again, he needed steel plates inserted on opposite sides of the damaged vertebrae and bolted together. The damage was mostly on the left side. He faced having one bung leg for the rest of his life.

TIM'S FIRST FLIGHT

'While a schoolboy at Greymouth, I went sightseeing in a small plane with Dad, around the Haupiri area.'

But Tim's thoughts were only for his business, Luggate Game Packers. As he lay in his hospital bed in that first week, all he worried about was whether he would be out of hospital in time to attend the commissioning of his new ship at Port Chalmers. 'I've bust my back,' he told family and friends, 'but I've got to be right by next Wednesday.'

Tim's idea had been to use the ships – remodelled coasters called *Ranginui* and *Hotunui* – in a role never tried before. He saw them as venison motherships. This is how it worked: deer were shot from helicopters in the Fiordland mountains and carried, dangling on the end of a rope, to the ships' helipads. On board, they would be stored in a chiller or freezer. When the ship's hold was full, the cargo was taken to the road-end at Milford Sound for transport to a venison factory inland.

It was a brilliant and daring idea of Tim's – deer removed by helicopter, ship and truck from one of remotest and most rugged environments in the world. A couple of years before his Queenstown crash he had persuaded the national park board to give him sole rights to harvest the deer herds in the vastness of Fiordland. The park board

welcomed his radical plan because deer were causing enormous damage to the forest, shrublands and grasslands of the park. They were stuffing up a precious ecosystem. Till then, the only way of controlling the exploding deer population was through a government culling scheme. Teams of hunters on foot shot the deer, collected the tails as evidence and then left the carcasses to rot. Tim thought that was a terrible waste.

But now, with a broken back, how on earth could he possibly lead the

Deer carcasses barged ashore from the Ranginui *at Milford Sound are loaded on to trucks for the journey out to a processing plant. The tractor was fitted with a special boom so it could lift the carcasses off the pontoon.*

ambitious Fiordland operation? Only those close to him knew how determined he could be. The commissioning of the *Hotunui* went ahead as planned, while Tim lay in the spinal unit. A hospital patient in the 1960s was pretty well cut off from the outside world. Tim had other ideas. Bung leg or not, he could still talk, read and write. He set about turning his hospital bed and bedside cabinet into a mini-office. He got a phone put in at his bedside, and he also convinced the hospital staff of his need for a radio telephone. Otherwise, he said, the lives of his helicopter crews might be at risk. A radio aerial was strung up outside his window and his brother, George, provided a spare radio set. At that time, from a base at Luggate, near Wanaka, his operation covered most of Fiordland and Mount Aspiring National Parks and adjacent mountain lands – by far the wildest corner of mainland New Zealand.

The coaster Hotunui *on commissioning day at Port Chalmers, July 1968. Two Luggate Game Packers helicopters demonstrated the loading of deer carcasses on to the ship's helipad.* Otago Daily Times

Tim was determined to get back into the action down south as soon as he could. He followed doctors' orders – well, up to a point. One piece of advice had to do with his water works. He was told to drink heaps to keep his bladder functioning well. In addition to hospital water, he thought beer would do him good. Old school mates like Robert Wilson and Mark Acland would wheel him to the local pub, a few hundred metres from the hospital, on the kind of raised table used in an operating theatre. His friends pushed him along the road, with motorists giving them strange looks. There was a urine bottle slung underneath the table.

At the pub, they lined Tim up at the bar. Clad in a hospital gown and lying face down, he had to lift his head off the pillow to drink his beer. Nearby, an older woman could not resist commenting:

'What have you done, dear?'

'Broken my back,' said Tim. 'Here,

Tim at his mother's home following his discharge from Christchurch Hospital. He is holding his catheter bottle. A calliper was later fitted to his paralysed left leg.

see for yourself.' And with that he untied the back of the gown and threw it open, baring not only a 20 centimetre-long scar on his back, but also his buttocks. The startled woman spilt her drink.

After two months Tim was discharged from hospital. His left leg was floppy. His right leg had lost some feeling but

ON THE 1968 CRASH

'A broken back and one bung leg weren't going to stop me.'

at least it would support him. To stand and have any hope of walking, he had to strap a steel calliper to his left leg. The frame extended from thigh to foot, and wrapped under his shoe. Hinged behind the knee, it clicked straight so he could stand and walk, limping, with his left leg stiff. To sit down he had to manually 'break' the calliper. 'I'm a walking paraplegic,' he told his friends.

While still recuperating at his mother's house in Christchurch, Tim got the news that a second Hiller helicopter in his fleet had been wrecked while chasing deer in Fiordland. Miraculously, pilot Bill Black (Blackie) and shooter Errol Brown survived. But it was another blow to Tim's business. Half the Luggate fleet of four helicopters had gone in less than three months.

Tim's accountant and closest advisor, Reid Jackson came to see him. Reid looked serious. He had reviewed Luggate's books. The company was in 'financial strife'. Tim had spent a small fortune on ships and helicopters, Reid said – and the company could go bankrupt.

That advice made Tim even more determined. He had to get back into a leading role. It was the only way to save his business.

A WILD WET PLACE

Fiordland is both awesome and weird to the eye – a region where ancient glaciers have carved shockingly steep rock walls, where the tannin-stained surface water of the fiords is the colour of weak tea, and where the mountains stream with waterfalls after a downpour. These really are mountains of water. Fiordland, one of the world's wettest regions, is a reception centre for moisture-laden weather systems radiating from the Southern Ocean. They crash into the mountains and drop their wet bundle as rain or snow. Too tough a place for farming or settlement on any scale, Fiordland became a national park in 1952 and a World Heritage Area in 1986. It's a huge area, 225 km long by up to 80 km wide. Only one sealed road crosses it – the Milford road.

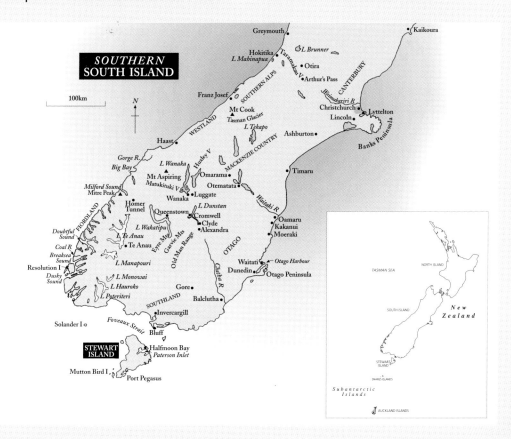

Tim flying his Hughes 500D helicopter ZK-HOT in the 'Campbell's Kingdom' gorge near Doubtful Sound, Fiordland.

Blackie agreed to take his boss into a remote part of Fiordland. Tim really wasn't fit enough yet. They flew to the mountains around Charles Sound, where one of Tim's deer recovery teams was working. On a grassy area high up, he ordered Blackie to let him out. The temptation was too much for Tim. There was a heap of deer there that needed gutting. He wanted to get stuck in. Blackie hovered the helicopter long enough for Tim to get out and as the Hiller lifted away, the rotor wash blew Tim over. When Blackie next looked back at the heap of deer, there was Tim lying across the wet moss and tussock grass, gutting the deer like a man possessed and desperate to contribute.

After a few more months of getting used to the calliper and building up strength in his good leg, Tim reckoned he was ready to fly a helicopter again – at least to try to. He asked Bill Black to give him a go. They chose spacious Oreti Beach near Invercargill for a test flight. A pilot normally needed two feet working the two pedals. Tim had only one good foot but Blackie had an idea. He tied Tim's right foot to the right pedal with a piece of baling twine. Now Tim could push and pull the right pedal. This meant that when he pulled it up, the left pedal went down.

Tim brought the Hiller to a hover several times before gently nudging it forward. In no time he had the machine speeding over the dunelands, good as gold. Bill saw the look of intense concentration on Tim's face turn into a huge smile of relief and pleasure. Tim knew he would soon be back in the air and going for it. He needed to be. He had a new frontier to tame. It would come to be known as New Zealand's Last Great Adventure.

The Wallis home in Geraldine
Street, Greymouth. The family's
1947 Chevrolet car is parked in
the street.

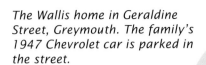

Tim swapped a chainsaw for t
350cc Royal Enfield motorcycl
He made use of it during schoc
holidays in 1956, his last year
Christ's College.

CHAPTER 2

A COASTER AT CHRIST'S COLLEGE

AIRCRAFT WEREN'T A BIG deal to Tim in his childhood. Helicopters had only just been invented and very little was known about them in New Zealand. Nor were deer and the hunting of them major talking points in his family. He grew up on the West Coast, at Greymouth, the second of four children. His father, Arthur Wallis, and his Uncle Norman were in the timber and sawmilling business. They owned several mills on the Coast which turned out timber from native trees such as rimu and kahikatea.

Timothy William Wallis was born on 9 September 1938. When he was a toddler the family moved to Geraldine Street, on the southern outskirts of Greymouth. His parents bought a stylish two-storey house with enough bedrooms for a growing family, and for a youngster who wanted to explore the bigger world as soon as he could walk, Geraldine Street was an adventure waiting to happen. On one side of the Wallis property was half an acre of bush. A good-sized stream called Sawyers Creek marked the southern boundary, and a smaller stream ran right through the property. A bush reserve across the road, filled with ferns and supplejack vines, was a glorious jungle to Tim, his older brother George, younger brother Adrian and sister Josephine.

Inside the house the Wallises displayed their family treasures, including an Indian tiger skin, complete with taxidermied head, shot by a great uncle of Tim's. The skin had a bullet hole about the region of the animal's heart. Family folklore said the tiger clawed the shooter's arm as it died.

Tim as a pre-schooler, with his younger brother, Adrian.

Their father spent long hours travelling on mill business. Sometimes Tim would go with him in his large Buick car, which he replaced in the 1940s with an equally large Chevrolet, also American made. There were many stops along the way for supplies and timber orders and visiting characters such as 'Peter the Pirate', a retired bushman who lived in a hermit's hut.

When Tim went to Christchurch with his mother in the train, which ran under the Southern Alps through the Otira Tunnel, he would walk along the aisle of the carriage trying to chat with everyone – a likeable blue-eyed little boy with a shock of fair hair parted on the right.

Tim started primary school at Grey Main in 1943, when the Second World War was still on. There were air-raid shelters in the school grounds and a large red cross on the roof of the local hospital in case Japanese warplanes somehow mounted an attack through Australia or the Western Pacific Islands. For exercise – and in recognition of the war effort – the children were marched in their classes, out the school gates and around the block, with brass-band music blaring from a wind-up gramophone. Tim's dad was excused from military service overseas because his work – timber production – was judged to be an 'essential industry'.

Tim, his brothers and sister biked about one kilometre to school. They biked home for lunch. In their spare time they often cycled with friends to other parts of town – down to the wharf to see the ships, to the signal station at the end of the breakwater, to the aerodrome. They built tree huts, explored the bush across the road, and caught eels in Sawyers Creek. Sometimes the eels were cooked and fed to the hens; sometimes they were dissected at the back door with Tim's grandfather's veterinary instruments. Tim loved seeing an eel's beating heart.

Arthur Wallis taught the children common courtesies and manners. For Sunday dinner, the boys would have to wear a jacket and tie. They were expected to stand up when a woman entered the room. He insisted on the children doing their homework when they came in from school and before they headed out to play. By the end of his Standard One year, Tim was described in a report as 'a good worker' who was 'very quick but must improve in neatness'.

For Christmas holidays the Wallises usually packed up their car and drove

Choir boys: Tim (left) and his brother, Adrian, were members of the local Anglican Church choir during their primary school years.

THOUGHTS ON NATIVE FOREST

In his last year at primary school, Tim wrote an essay titled, 'Why We Must Not Destroy Our Native Forest'. The forest, he wrote, protected river banks from erosion and provided habitat and food for native birds. He mentioned that introduced animals like deer and possums damaged native forest. He also noted that the forest provided 'essential' timber for building houses.

off over Arthur's Pass (the Haast highway had yet to be opened) for a holiday at Wanaka or at Queenstown with Tim's Aunt Betsy, his mother's younger sister, who was his godmother. Betsy and her husband ran a boat-hire business for visitors to Queenstown. In 1947, at the age of nine, Tim took a precious gift on the Christmas holiday – a spring-loaded BSA air-gun.

At Queenstown that year, down by the boats, he met a Dunedin boy of similar age, Robert Wilson. It was the start of a life-long friendship. To enliven the moment Tim had an idea for a shooting competition. Back at his aunt's place, the two boys took turns at knocking over match boxes with shots from the air-gun. When that proved easy enough they competed to see who could light the matches. To do that, the slug had to strike the match-head very exactly.

Tim's first time in an aeroplane was around 1950 when he took a flight with his dad from Greymouth Airport in a small aircraft. They flew to the Grey Valley for a look over the native forest that supplied his dad's Kopara sawmill.

Young Tim Wallis liked to experiment with lots of things. He played around with chemicals that converted shiny black West Coast coal into a substance that looked like tropical coral, coloured pink, white and blue. Approaching his teenage years, he also experimented with explosives. The pharmacy in town sold the basic ingredients to Tim and his mates. You just had to know the names of the chemicals. During a school holiday, Tim and his brother Adrian, who also loved chemical experiments, asked their mother if there was anything they could do in the garden. She said they

Holiday time at Queenstown. From left are Adrian, Josephine, Belinda Wilson, her brother Robert Wilson, and Tim. They were photographed by the Steamer Wharf boat-hire business run by Tim's godmother, Aunt Betsy and her husband.

AUNT BETSY

An inspiration to Tim, Aunt Betsy was a mountaineering sensation. She became a guide at Mount Cook village when she was 18 – an unusual job for a woman – and made a first ascent of Mt Oates in Arthur's Pass National Park at the age of 21. When Tim was 10, she took him over the Routeburn Track and to the top of The Remarkables, the highest mountains close to Queenstown.

could fix the broken concrete steps down to Sawyers Creek if they liked. 'No sooner said than done, Mum,' was the boys' reply.

The next thing she heard was an explosion. Then the phone rang. A neighbour told her he'd nearly been hit on the head by a flying piece of concrete. Janice Wallis was annoyed but Tim merely said: 'Good, that experiment was a success then!'

The last report on Tim from his primary school read: '… needs confidence in himself building up.'

The place where that would happen was the prestigious private boarding school, Christ's College in Christchurch.

Because both his father's family and his mother's had sent boys to Christ's College, Tim was the third generation in his family to be enrolled there. The Wallises were reasonably well off but hardly rich. Unlike the sons of wealthy Canterbury landowners he was now rubbing shoulders with, Tim's inheritance wasn't going to be in the form of land or money. It was more to do with abstract things like being enterprising and determined enough to push through visionary ideas. He admired his father's leadership qualities. He, too, saw himself at the leading edge of things – wherever and whatever that might be.

In some ways Christ's was a rude awakening for the new boarder. Following in his father's footsteps, Tim joined School House. The routines were traditional and inescapable. Caning – a number of whacks on the backside with a cane stick – might follow any breach or shirking of the rules. Here's an idea of the daybreak routine:

- Out of bed smartly at 6.30 am.
- Down the wooden staircase in a dressing gown to the concrete-floored bathroom at ground level, a fridge in winter.
- A quick dip in a communal bath of running cold water.
- Then into school uniform and away to the dining room where breakfast was eaten from polished wooden tables.

The college's main buildings, dating from 1850, were formed around a quadrangle. The stonework exteriors, with ornate appendages, are still there, looking like they were erected for a film set of Harry Potter's Hogwarts.

After breakfast, church. There was always a service in the stain-glassed and stone-clad chapel. The Bible readings and

ON CANING . . .

'I was caught sneaking around when I should have been in bed. Seven strokes. It hurt.'

At Christ's College in Tim's day, the juniors did chores for the seniors. The younger boys might clean shoes or make beds or go to the tuck-shop to buy something for the senior students they were assigned to. The practice, imported from English schools, was called fagging. Tim, when in the sixth form, wrote home: '...I get my bed made just like you do in a hotel.' Soon after he left, fagging was phased out at Christ's.

a hymn or two lasted about 15 minutes, six days a week and twice on Sundays. After chapel, tuition. Teachers at Christ's were either 'masters' or 'tutors' – never ordinary old 'teachers'. Tim's house master was also the headmaster – Harry Reginald Hornsby. The boys called him 'Harry' although not to his face. He had a profound influence on Christ's and many of the boys, challenging them to read more widely and become interested in international affairs and politics. Many of the boys, including Tim, found Mr Hornsby inspiring, and he brought out the best in them. Years later, Tim would be one of the pallbearers at Reg Hornsby's funeral, and the old headmaster would bequeath to Tim a silver-handled walking stick.

For the time being however, Tim concentrated on adapting to college life. He made friends easily and enjoyed the communal nature of boarding school. He wasn't a star student, although he excelled at certain subjects. Biology was one. In maths, a fourth-form report described him as 'capable but rather slapdash'. Physics theory: 'only fair'. Physics practical was a different story, especially outside the classroom. He made pistols – .22-calibre, with the handle made of

aluminium from a wooden mould. He and a friend put a lot of thought into the manufacture and function of the firing pin. The school had a metalwork shop but there were parts that required lathing or welding that could only be done in the city. He tried out the pistol on a friend's farm, scaring the blazes out of the rabbits and an occasional hare.

Tim was always building or fixing things. He repaired a broken chainsaw from his father's sawmill in the Grey

Tim (centre left with headgear and striped jersey) in action for the Christ's College rugby First XV against Otago Boys' High School at the Otago Boys' ground, Dunedin, 1956. Lock Tom Hutchinson is catching the ball. Christ's won 11–3. Otago Daily Times

HITCHING A RAILCAR RIDE

This is a story about a 15-year-old boy who stopped a railcar to get a lift home. After a school dance in Christchurch one night, Tim asked a school mate, Mark Acland, who had his father's car and was licensed to drive, to give him a lift to the railway station. Tim knew he had only minutes to get the late railcar service to Greymouth. Mark planted his foot and off they sped down the main shopping street of Christchurch, Colombo Street. Suddenly, a policeman with a torch signalled them to stop. Tim wound down his window and explained they were desperately late for the Coast railcar. 'Then you'll have to hurry, sonny,' said the cop. And off they sped, boy racers of the '50s, only to find the railcar pulling out of the station. Tim directed Mark to drive the long street parallel to the tracks to get ahead of the railcar. After a few blocks they turned left towards a level crossing, Tim got out with his bag and, standing in the middle of the tracks, illuminated by the railcar's lights, waved madly. The driver recognised him as one of the West Coast students and slammed on the brakes. Which is how Tim got home that night.

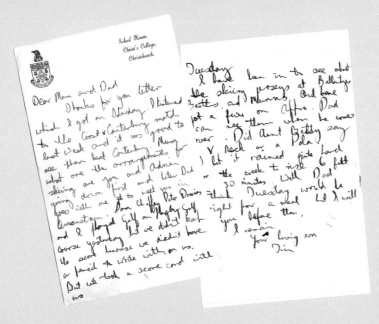

Valley and suddenly his first business opportunity opened up. He wanted a motorbike. During the school holidays he advertised in the *Greymouth Evening Star*: 'Wanted to swap: chainsaw for motorbike.' A man came around to Geraldine Street with a Royal Enfield 350cc bike. It was a deal. And from that deal came another when he sold the motorbike and bought a car, an old Austin sorely in need of repairs. No problem.

Nor was there a problem making a bomb in his fifth-form year. It was right up his alley.

All it took was a bit of chemistry, much of which he'd learnt before his teens, combined with a little physics. He and a friend got some white blasting powder and rigged up a bomb using a steel soda siphon pressure cartridge and a two-minute length of fuse. At a quiet moment they took it down to the school swimming pool and … 'There was a tremendous explosion,' said Tim. 'We didn't wait to see the results … we were in the [botanic] gardens in no time!' That evening school mates said they'd seen a column of white smoke shoot into the air.

Then there was the time Tim blew up

the college quadrangle. Well, not quite. In the dead of night, around 2 am, he convinced a friend to throw a Nescafé coffee tin filled with a bomb mixture and flashing powder into the quadrangle from an upstairs window. There was a mighty bang. It made a small hole in one corner of the quadrangle. Many of the boys and a few masters were woken up by it. At assembly in the morning, the boys responsible for the explosion were asked to come forward. Tim got six strokes of the cane on the backside for being the instigator (in those days they'd call that 'six of the best'). His friend also got caned.

Tim was caned for other stuff. He was caught once sneaking around the dormitory, after lights-out. He'd write home about these incidents, but he rarely complained about the punishments. The college expected the boys to write

RELUCTANT PREFECT

In his last year at college, Tim was appointed a prefect. 'I don't enjoy being a school prefect very much,' he wrote home, 'but I suppose I will get over that.'

home once a week and Tim took that duty seriously. Often he would request something – more of mum's jams, cakes and cordial drinks. Or clothes and sometimes ski gear. In winter there was skiing at the Mt Cheeseman field in the Canterbury mountains. Introduced to skiing at Coronet Peak by his Aunt Betsy (who was a New Zealand representative in 1950), Tim was soon in the college ski team. He threw himself at the sport. After one weekend at Mt Cheeseman he wrote a letter home about '… going very fast out of control … did an eggbeater into the snow. It's good doing a decent spill, it's all in the game.'

Academically Tim knuckled down and in 1955 he won a school prize in mathematics and continued to do well in biology and geography. His biology teacher, announcing he was top of his class said Tim 'thoroughly deserves his position'. Headmaster Hornsby wrote 'as usual, cheerful and busy.'

At college, Tim played golf, squash and tennis. He also rowed, swam and boxed. But rugby, called 'football' then, and skiing were his main sports. He packed down in the First XV scrum as a flanker or No. 8. By his last year at college, 1956, Tim was a big lad. He'd put on 25 kg at college, and now weighed 80 kg and stood 1.83 m (6 feet) tall. That season Christ's won every match except one, which was drawn.

His rugby coach and School House tutor, Zane Dalzell, summed up his last year at college – 'He'd give everything a go.'

Five years at Christ's College confirmed Tim's ability to seize opportunities and push limits. The friends he had made there would be friends for life – today Tim is godfather to 17 children of his ex-Christ's College friends. In every way the school had made an enduring mark on the young man. 'We will miss him very much,' wrote his house master, to which headmaster Reg Hornsby added, 'He possesses an independent mind'.

The Wallis quartet – George, Tim, Adrian and Josephine.

Tim deer-stalking at the head of a South Westland valley in the 1960s.

CHAPTER 3

DEER-STALKING AFTER WORK

TIM LEFT COLLEGE with University Entrance – 'accredited', he told his parents, 'and I am pleased because I don't think I deserved it'. But he was unsure what lay ahead – work or study? He reckoned he wasn't cut out for academic studies. To Tim, it meant an 'indoors life'. It wasn't for him. He'd rather go farming.

His mum encouraged him to go to medical school and become a doctor. His dad pictured him with a career in the timber industry. Pushing between these two views, like a referee, was the military. It ordered Tim to attend a training course at Burnham camp south of Christchurch. A hangover from the Second World War, military training for school-leavers was compulsory. No arguments.

With a Christ's College and West Coast friend, Richard Coates, Tim drove his Austin 7 car over Arthur's Pass to the Canterbury Plains and Burnham. But on the Christchurch side of Otira, where the mountains get very steep, the little car ran out of puff. Refusing to hitch a ride, Tim simply turned it around and backed it up the last few bends to the summit using its super-low reverse gear.

At Burnham he joined an artillery unit, although he had earlier thought air force training might be better. He got to fire 25-pounder field guns and drive up to six different vehicle types in one day. Already familiar with boarding school discipline, Tim made the most of the Burnham environment, although he told his family that the discipline was 'so strict in parts it becomes stupid'. In the interests of fitness he quit smoking, which he'd only recently taken up in a minor way.

Tim (left) and Sam Satterthwaite were part of the 21st Compulsory Military Training (CMT) intake at the Burnham camp, south of Christchurch.

After ten weeks at Burnham, he tried his mother's idea of a career in medicine but lasted just two terms at Canterbury University. He found the studies 'pretty tough'. Now it was his dad's turn to sort out a pathway for him. As the boss at the big Kopara sawmill in the Grey Valley, Arthur Wallis had no trouble finding a job for Tim. All the same, he showed his 18-year-old son no favours. Tim started at the bottom rung – 'whistle boy'. His job was to make sure the snigger, who roped up the fallen logs, and the winchman, who hauled them out, were in communication with each other. From whistle boy Tim became a 'slabbie', responsible for disposing of the waste wood around the mill. It was a job, but nowhere near challenging enough for Tim. He looked to the mountain tops for a challenge – deerstalking. Just about all his spare time was devoted to it.

With a few mates, Tim would head up to the treeline after work or at weekends. Rugby fit, he could canter up hills with a light pack and a .303 Lee Enfield rifle. On a warm night, he might sleep out in the tussock and make it back to the mill in the morning for the start of a new working day. He felt so happy in the remoteness of the mountains, where a hunter had to be self-sufficient. If anything went wrong, help was a long way off.

Deer-stalking for Tim was all about testing yourself against an animal that could hear and smell – and possibly see – better than you. It was about honing your senses and being cleverer than the animal. When you found deer tracks, you had to be able to follow them. In the end, stalking the deer was the main point of the sport. Pulling the trigger was but the end of the experience; it wasn't always the finest moment. A famous American naturalist and writer, Henry David Thoreau, put it this way: 'Men go fishing all their lives without knowing that it is not fish they are after.'

But Tim and his mates did shoot quite a lot of red deer – Tim called them 'redskins' – which they carried out on their backs. They'd bone out the venison meat on the river flats, then they'd wrap it in cheese cloth and sell it to a butchery near Greymouth for a shilling a pound (in the old money and weight measures). The venison was mostly blended into sausages.

From the mill job, Tim joined the Forest Service for a while. It was a

FIRST DEER

Tim was motorbiking on a lonely back-country road on the Coast when he shot his first deer. A young stag strolled out of the bush in front of him. He slammed on the brakes, spun around and grabbed his rifle, and fired. Down went the deer. Tim was quivering with excitement, hardly knowing what to do next. He slung the deer across the bike's petrol tank and went off with it to the Kopara sawmill, enormously proud of himself.

Tim operating the tractor he used for his manuka firewood project near Hamilton, 1960.

cruisy job – literally. His task, known as 'cruising', was to measure and catalogue trees in a government-owned forest for their timber value. It kept him super fit. Not surprisingly, when he took up rugby with the Star club in Greymouth, Tim was good enough to get into the West Coast team. At 19, he was probably the youngest player ever to represent the region – a big broad-shouldered lad, a loose forward with speed to burn.

Tim's father, eyeing up logging and sawmilling opportunities in the Haast area far to the south, could see work opening up for Tim and his brother George in the future. He urged Tim to get more experience in the industry. He was now 20. Over the next 15 months he took two jobs in the timber industry.

The first was at Timaru, for Desmond Unwin Ltd, where he sorted timber into lots for house construction and other uses. In his spare time he played rugby at club level and soon made the South Canterbury side. The highlight was taking on Canterbury at Lancaster Park (now Jade Stadium). But by mid-season he felt 'brassed off with foot-ball... it's starting to tie me down.' He'd missed out on a wallaby shoot because he was required for rugby practice and 'it mucked a whole Sunday up.' Skiing appealed to him more than rugby. When he declined an opportunity to play for the South Island against the North Island, it put the skids on his rugby career.

From Timaru, now 21, Tim went to Hamilton at the beginning of 1960 to work for another timber merchant. He handled orders. He knew he wouldn't last long at paperwork and he didn't. Within a couple of months he was looking for something different, thinking he might save up for an overseas trip. He advertised in a Hamilton newspaper for weekend work. A farmer replied. He wanted someone to drive a bulldozer at a quarry on his farm, and help clear a stand of native trees called manuka. Tim took the job. His eyes lit up at the sight of the manuka.

With a Christ's College friend, John Chapman, he bought a tractor and fitted a tray to the back of it with which to carry the sticks of manuka. The two friends worked 12-hour days at the weekends, and made good money selling the firewood. Less than four months after starting with the Hamilton timber merchants, Tim wrote to his parents:

'Do not send any mail to E & B (Ellis & Bernand) as I left today … 1) The pay isn't terribly much to save on to go overseas. 2) I was a timber orderman, which is all right for a while but it does not appeal to me.' At the end of the

Tim, in a hard hat, and his brother George at Ross, 1960. George is driving a hired TD9 International.

CHAT ON A BRIDGE

In the early 1960s, Max Kershaw was the New Zealand Forest Service ranger who looked after animal control operations throughout Otago and Southland. One day, he and a government deer culler were crossing a bridge over the Haast River on foot. A green International log truck roared towards them. The truck stopped halfway and the passenger leaned out to have a chat. It was Tim Wallis. They had heard of Tim. For about 15 minutes the Forest Service men and Tim talked of deer, how many there were and how the deer control programme was going. As the log truck pulled away, the two men on foot noticed an impressive pile of deer carcasses lying on top of the logs.

letter he wrote: 'This is nothing to be disappointed about.'

But Tim knew his parents, especially his dad, would be disappointed. Maybe downright wild. His dad might think Tim was turning his back on the timber trade and a Wallis family heritage. But they also knew that Tim loved the southern mountains and longed to be near them. Hamilton was like another country compared to the Coast.

So Tim came home. His brother, George – the two were best mates – found some logging work for the two of them near the town of Ross. In the near future, George could see a new frontier for timber opening up around Haast, aided by the completion of the Haast Pass road between Westland and Otago shortly before Christmas 1960. It meant the plentiful South Westland native timber could get to southern New Zealand. The brothers hatched a scheme. George would organise the logging and trucking of the logs over the Haast Pass to the township of Luggate, near Wanaka. Tim would manage a sawmill there under a lease arrangement with its owner, and market the timber. So Haast Timbers Ltd was born.

Essentially, the logs came out of a

Tim's friends Robert Wilson and Mark Acland with three shot deer near Rainbow Valley, Mount Aspiring National Park in the 1960s.

remote rainforest region by way of a narrow, winding gravel road, steep and landslide-prone in places, across a low pass (562 m above sea level) in the Southern Alps, then on into the dry brown landscape of Central Otago, where the logs were turned into sawn timber.

Tim worked hard at selling the timber. In his spare time he'd go deer-stalking.

His childhood mate, Robert Wilson, would often drive up from Dunedin on a Friday night to join him. They'd trek into the mountains under moonlight and make camp high up in order to be ready for the hunting at sunrise, often the best time. They sold venison to a Wanaka butcher and a Christchurch restaurant, and they'd sell antlers or velvet to Chinese laundries in Christchurch for the oriental medicine trade in China. On some deer-stalking trips, Tim and his mates would come across huge mobs of deer, which set Tim thinking. The deer plague was causing extensive damage to the forest and grasslands of the South Island. Something radical needed to be done to control their escalating numbers, and Tim, being Tim, saw not just a problem, but an opportunity. He started thinking about harvesting the venison on a large scale.

So while marketing timber, Tim began to quietly dabble in the venison trade. The log trucks on the Haast Pass road would pick up carcasses from individual hunters at pre-arranged depots. The deer were carried on top of the logs and brought to Luggate for processing, and Tim paid the hunters later.

But one difficulty occupied Tim's mind. Carcasses came out of the mountains in a variety of ways – by packhorse, Landrover, motorboat and light planes that used hair-raising airstrips hacked out of the bush. Otherwise, the hunter had to carry the carcass out on his back. There had to be a better way. What was needed was a means of bridging the gap between the open mountain country, where the deer could be harvested in huge numbers, and the nearest road. Tim wrestled with the problem. Then he had a thought.

Would helicopters do the trick?

CHAPTER 4

'LORD OF THE CHOPPERS'

THE HELICOPTER HIRED to test the idea of heli-harvesting of deer arrived in bits on a trailer. It looked like a giant toy meccano set waiting to be assembled. How could such an ungainly jumble of bits and pieces possibly fly?

Magically, the trailer load turned into a Bell 47 D1 helicopter, a model used by American forces in the Korean War in the 1950s. In New Zealand it came to be known as the Mash chopper after it appeared in the television series *MASH*, featuring life in an American medical unit in the Korean War. The chopper was hired by Tim, his friend Robert Wilson and a top deer hunter, Wattie Cameron. They leased it from a Nelson firm, together with its American pilot, Milton Stills.

Tim and Robert were the business brains behind the trial in April 1963. They wanted to know if a helicopter could transport the deer efficiently out of the back country and make a profit. On the next available weekend they called together a team of 11 shooters and headed up the Matukituki Valley near Wanaka. It was like an army exercise. Timing was everything. Mobs of deer were driven from the grassy mountain tops towards an ambush. Over 200 were shot that day. The helicopter ferried the carcasses on its side racks, a few at a time, to a road on the valley floor. Trucks took them on to Wanaka for processing, then to Dunedin for shipping to markets in Germany. Robert Wilson had arranged the deal. Gale-force winds grounded the helicopter late in the day but by then it had transported 110 deer, enough for the trial.

Tim and Robert did the sums. They'd made a profit, if only just. Forget the

Tim and his aunt, Betsy Ensor, talking to a cattle musterer in the Okuru Valley during a deer-stalking trip in the 1960s.

motorboats and bush planes, there was a whole industry waiting to be launched on the back of helicopters!

A syndicate of shooters led by Tim and Robert hired a second chopper from Nelson and put it to work in the mountains around Wanaka. But they had to work damned hard for long hours (4 am to 10 pm some days) to cover the hire charges. Tim's solution to this was simple: he needed his own helicopter, perhaps more than one, and he needed to be able to fly them in pursuit of deer.

As for the timber business at Luggate, he and George were in the process of selling out to a big Auckland company. Their father had died a couple of years earlier and Tim felt his future lay in deer more than in timber. He and an old West Coast mate, Geoff Taylor, had already set up a chiller for storing deer meat. In 1964, they built a small venison factory. It would be the foundation of a firm called Luggate Game Packers.

In 1965, Tim bought his first helicopter, a Bell 47 G4. It cost £18,530, a lot of money then, and he paid a deposit of £3,000. The balance he borrowed from a bank, using his mother to guarantee the loan. Then he arranged to get lessons

. . . .
EARLY CHOPPERS

American expeditions to Antarctica in 1946–47 and through the 1950s brought the first helicopters to New Zealand. They were large lumbering Sikorskys. The first helicopters registered in New Zealand were assigned to farm work – spraying and fencing.

The first helicopter recovery of deer, in the mountains above the Matukituki Valley, April 1963. Robert Wilson is dragging a stag towards the hired Bell 47 for airlifting to the road-end on the valley floor. Otago Daily Times

on how to fly the Bell 47 from John Reid, the Nelson instructor who headed Helicopters New Zealand.

In those days, you first had to learn to fly an ordinary plane before you learnt to fly a helicopter. John Reid, the instructor, sent Tim off to the Canterbury Aero Club at Christchurch, where he got his licence in three weeks flying a Piper 140 Cherokee. John was astonished at how quickly Tim did things. He was a fast learner, no question. In the helicopter Tim soon mastered take-off, landing and level flight and he put in extra hours for experience in mountain flying.

Heading back to Wanaka, he picked up his mother, Janice, at Christchurch. 'Cross your fingers for a fine weekend,' he'd told her. On her knees she had a map of the route ahead and at her feet was a large can of petrol in case they ran out of fuel. By the time they'd reached South Canterbury a north-westerly gale was raging so Tim landed at a friend's farm near Omarama. Next day they arrived at Luggate and landed in a paddock near Tim's cottage. People came from all over the district to see the marvellous new machine in their midst, and Tim took a few of them for joy-rides.

Road-end in the Matukituki Valley for the first helicopter shoot, April 1963. The shoot used a Bell 47 helicopter. Bernard Pinney

But joy-riding was not what he'd bought the chopper for. He put it to work right away, flying shooters to a place where deer were known to be in good numbers and returning a few hours later to pick up whatever they'd shot. Over the next week or so, his factory put through far more venison than before.

Then, disaster struck. Ten days after arriving back with the Bell 47, Tim was dropping two shooters up the Matukituki Valley when the machine lurched backwards on landing. The tail rotor struck rocks and the helicopter quickly heeled over and thrashed itself to a standstill. It was a total wreck.

Back at the Luggate factory, the

DRAMA AT DUSK

There were never enough hours of daylight for Tim. He became well known for flying at dusk when most pilots would think twice about doing that. One summer's day, he dropped off his friend, Robert Wilson high up in the mountains west of Wanaka so Robert could go hunting deer. By the evening, Robert had shot six deer and was waiting at a pre-arranged spot for Tim to return to pick him up. As the sun went down it became cold. Wearing just a singlet and shorts, Robert crawled inside a gutted deer carcass to keep himself warm. Then, with the light fading, Tim flew over the rendezvous site but couldn't see his friend anywhere. He went away for a few minutes and came back to find Robert scrambling out of the carcass and waving his arms frantically. On the flight home, Tim's passenger smelt something awful...

manager Jim Faulks heard a vehicle pull up and then the door opened. Tim stood there, blood spattered over his shirt from a nick in his left ear.

'Jim,' he said quietly, 'we've had an accident. The helicopter's not too good.' The nick in the ear would be a permanent reminder of his first chopper crash.

Luckily, Tim and the shooters had got off lightly. Although the helicopter was insured, he was now in serious debt, had just had a major accident and was damned lucky to have escaped major injury. His mother and some friends thought he should consider quitting. Tim had other ideas.

During the following years, deer recovery methods changed. Chopper became gunship. With the door removed, a shooter fired at the deer from the air instead of from the ground. One chopper crew downed 248 deer in one day in the Shotover catchment behind Queenstown. And soon deer weren't loaded on racks mounted on the side of the helicopter; they were tied together and carted out on a sling hooked underneath the machine. In addition to the shooter, the venison choppers also carried a crewman whose job was to

The wreckage of Tim's first helicopter, a Bell 47, in the Leaping Burn, Matukituki Valley. Robert Wilson (left) was among those who went up to take photos for the insurance assessment.

gut the fallen animals. The gutter had to jump out of the machine, often onto steep, uneven ground. Sometimes he would be given a lift to the next site while riding the rope under the helicopter. It was a hazardous job – not an option these days for safety reasons.

With deer becoming scarce in the brownish mountain country east of the Southern Alps, Tim turned his attention

- -
ON HELICOPTER CRASHES ...

'Helicopters do go boom when they hit the ground, and they bust up something terrible.'

THE 'FLYING JEEP'

The helicopter is such a handy aircraft. It can fly straight up or down or in any direction, including sideways. It can also hover. But how does it do all this? Its design, size and weight, like the bumblebee's, suggest it is defying natural laws.

Invented in the 1930s, the helicopter is propelled by a rotating set of long narrow blades – typically two to four in a set – that are attached to a central hub. The main rotor blades, which can be angled, grip the air, and when the hub and blades are tipped, the helicopter will move in whatever direction is signalled by the pilot using a stick called a cyclic. With one hand the pilot moves the cyclic; with the other he/she will manoeuvre a lever called the collective, which moves the helicopter up or

Jim Faulks and Tim Wallis on a deer survey in Fiordland in 1966. This was before the crash near Queenstown, which broke Tim's back and paralysed his left leg. Jock Murdoch

down by changing the angle (pitch) of the blades. It also applies power to the engine, up or down, according to the demand put on it.

At a hover the helicopter has a cushion of air beneath it. Moving forward (with the main rotor hub tipped forward), it has to get out of a zone of turbulent air before it will fly efficiently.

Because the main rotor blades all turn in the same direction, the body of the helicopter naturally wants to begin spinning wildly. To avoid crashing, helicopters must counteract this force, called torque. Most do this through a small rotor mounted on the tail. This acts as a propeller to give stability and steerage.

Able to fly in any direction and land on reasonably flat surfaces, the helicopter is immensely versatile and used for all sorts of work. When it first became involved in deer recovery, it was nicknamed the 'Flying Jeep'.

to wild, green Fiordland. The terrain and climate there were a lot tougher for helicopters. 'Tiger country' is what crews called it. And the weather could be downright dangerous. High winds and downdrafts were very troublesome for choppers. But deer were plentiful. They were so plentiful they were causing huge damage to the forest, the native wildlife and the grasslands above the treeline. Could Tim get the deer out? Without refuelling, the Hiller helicopters in his fleet couldn't fly from Te Anau to the remote ocean side of Fiordland and back again with a load of deer. The region was just too big.

The Tim Wallis solution: fly the shot deer to a ship based in the fiords. Two choppers, if they had a good run, would fill the holds in a few days. This exercise would revolutionise venison recovery in Fiordland and boost his business beyond the imaginings of most other operators.

About this time Tim's operation became controversial. There were other hunters with access to helicopters, called 'meat hawks', who wanted a crack at the Fiordland deer. Tim argued for sole rights to harvest the bulk of the national park. He said he'd invest in ships if he got sole rights. The Fiordland National

Tim hovers a Hiller 12E high up in the East Branch of the Matukituki Valley as Joe Cave hooks on a load of deer. Robert Wilson

Park board, which decided on these things, agreed with Tim and awarded him a three-year contract.

That decision – and a renewal of the contract in 1970 – upset a few of his competitors. There was some poaching – opposition choppers trying to nick deer when no one was about. You could get away with it because Fiordland was such a big place. Some people said rifle shots were fired at helicopters. There were sabotage incidents – sand in the oil, for example, or water in the fuel. At the local pub in Te Anau, there were arguments and an occasional fist fight. A hangar near Te Anau owned by Tim's company, Alpine Helicopters, was set ablaze. The so-called 'Venison Wars' were in full swing. Air force Iroquois choppers appeared in Fiordland to try to restore the peace, and the police got involved. Flying helicopters in rugged terrain and dodgy weather was hazardous enough without the pilots and crews taking risks for the sake of rivalry. There had been numerous prangs, lots of injuries and some deaths.

Walking with a limp after breaking his back in the Queenstown crash in 1968, Tim tried not to get embroiled in the arguments. For one thing, he was too

THREAT OF POISONING

In a desperate bid to reduce deer numbers in the mountains near Lake Wanaka in the 1960s, the Government planned an aerial poisoning campaign involving 1080 poison. Carrots laced with 1080 were to be dropped across a large area by light planes based at Makarora. When Tim heard about this, he became very angry because he knew the 1080 would destroy a resource he was going to harvest with helicopters. To his mind that was an appalling waste. He travelled to Wellington to see senior people in the Government, including a Cabinet Minister. They were persuaded by his argument. The planned 1080 drop was abandoned.

busy building the business, and he was often in the air himself, checking out his expanding network of helicopters, trucks and processing facilities. Alpine Helicopters was now a big business, and Tim Wallis was a wealthy man. But that was no reason to relax! Tim knew he always had to be one step ahead of everyone else.

Towards the end of 1972, Alpine Helicopters acquired a flash new Bell Jet Ranger from America – the first chopper of its kind in southern New

Looking down Lake Wanaka. In the mid-1960s, Tim established a road between West Wanaka to Minaret Creek for early deer recovery by ground shooting. George Wallis

Zealand. It was a fast machine, capable of 195 kph under full load. More to the point, the new helicopter's range – how far it could travel on a tank of fuel – was far greater than the Hiller's.

The Bell Jet Ranger could gather up deer from the ocean side of Fiordland and return to a road-end on the eastern side. This made the motherships *Ranginui* and *Hotunui* all but redundant. Then the price of venison declined in 1973 by about two-thirds.

All this forced Tim and his board of directors to rethink their operation. The question they came up with was this: were red deer worth more dead or alive? Definitely the latter – deer farming had already begun, and it was about to become a significant industry. The challenge for Tim's company was to find efficient ways of capturing the wild deer alive and getting them out safely.

Alpine Helicopters' fleet grew in number and in horsepower. More Jet Rangers arrived – eight from Canada in one purchase, ten from America in another. Hughes 500 helicopters also joined the fleet.

An Alpine Helicopters' Bell Jet Ranger with a sling-load of deer, including some velvet antlers at the top. Malcolm Wheeler

By the mid-1970s, Tim had become 'Lord of the Choppers'. He didn't really care, though, how many helicopters his company owned. His life was all about moving from one challenging project to another. He loved a challenge and exploring new ways of doing things.

Capturing deer live in the mountains, and farming them, would preoccupy him through the next decade.

ON FLYING FOR DEER . . .

'The mountains were yours ...
Sometimes you had to stretch daylight a little.'

*Colin Yeates, standing on the skid of a Hughes 500, with a hand-held net gun,
on a cloudy day in Fiordland.*

*Opposite: Donald Greig riding the strop under Tim's helicopter with
a captured deer at the world deer farming congress at Mt Hutt in 1993.*

CHAPTER 5

AIRBORNE DEER

TIM'S HELICOPTER COMPANY was among the first to capture deer live from the wild. In the mid-1960s, dare-devil helicopter crewmen would leap on to the backs of moving deer and wrestle the terrified animals to a standstill like rodeo cowboys. It was called bull-dogging. Not for the faint-hearted, it usually resulted in bruises and sometimes broken limbs There had to be a better way.

In the first place there were drugs, injected into the running deer by a dart syringe fired from a specially designed pistol or rifle. Instead of using bullets, the heli-shooter fired darts. The drugs immobilised the deer, either by affecting its muscles or by tranquillising it.

In 1968, Tim responded to a request from Lincoln College near Christchurch, an agricultural university, for a truck load of red deer. Lincoln wanted the wild deer for an experiment to see how they could be domesticated and farmed. On the day before he broke his back near Queenstown, Tim flew to the Criffel Range near his Luggate base with two assistants – Lin Herron, a farmer from the Queenstown area, and Colin Murdoch, a pioneer in the live capture of wild animals. Deer tracks and the deer themselves were easily spotted in the snow, and the exercise was successful. Eight rather surprised deer were caught and trucked off to Lincoln.

The following year, Tim's chief pilot, Bill Black, and shooter Jim Kane

Opposite: Collecting breeding stock for Criffel Deer Farm.

developed a different method of live capture. Instead of using a pistol or rifle, the shooter wielded a bamboo pole with a syringe at the end. As Bill manoeuvred the chopper close to the fleeing deer, the shooter leant out with the pole and used it rather like a medieval knight jousting with a lance.

Then came the 'stun gun'. It delivered a mild electrical charge from helicopter to deer. A double-barrelled gun fired two darts towing live wires from the chopper. When they struck the deer, its muscles were immobilised by the electric current, and the animal stood on the spot, quivering. The shooter would jump out, strap its legs and get it into a bag for transporting to a road-end and deer farm.

Bamboo pole, stun gun, rifle-fired syringe – they all had their drawbacks as far as Tim was concerned. By the early 1970s, deer farming was growing in leaps and bounds, especially in southern New Zealand. Red deer had become the world's newest farm animal.

Tim looked around for improved methods for capturing wild stock. He seized on the idea of using nets fired from guns that were hand-held or mounted on the helicopter's skids. He

John Muir and Tim with deer captured by a skid-mounted net-gun on the slopes of the Criffel Range.

wasn't the first to use nets. A Hawkes Bay farmer, Gordon McNutt, in the late 1960s devised a net that was dropped on to a fleeing deer from the front of his helicopter. Then came a series of hand-held guns that fired nets. But the recoil from these was pretty bad, often leaving the shooter with cut hands or broken fingers. Finally, the skid-mounted net-gun was devised by two West Coasters, Ivan Wilson and Graham Jacobs. They called it the 'Gotcha Gun'. Clearly, its time had arrived because similar devices were being developed at Te Anau and Nelson.

Tim set up a workshop at Wanaka dedicated to the research and develop-ment of live-capture methods. He loved being at the leading edge of this and engaged people with engineering and electrical skills to work out the finer details. The skid-mounted net-guns could be triggered by the pilot instead of the shooter. This freed the shooter to be attending to a captured deer on the ground while the pilot flew off to find the next target.

Deer were intelligent enough to know to hide in the bush if they could. The live-capture business would often turn into a battle of wits. Deer versus pilot.

Tim and Prue on their wedding day, outside the Pretoria registry office.

Pilots became very skilled at flushing deer out of the bush and herding them into places where they could be netted. For many pilots this was the ultimate thrill, better than shooting to kill. It gave you all the daring and thrill-of-the-chase you needed and it ended with a wide-eyed deer riding in a bag under the chopper. It has been called New Zealand's Last Great Adventure – the harvesting of red deer, dead and now alive, from the wildest regions of New Zealand.

Tim was in the thick of it all. He liked being at the frontline – winging it through the cut and thrust of a chase. There was instant joy and achievement from netting a handsome hind whose progeny might one day win prizes for velvet antler and venison production. He liked, too, encouraging developments in net-gun design and testing helicopter models with each new design. The Hiller helicopters were phased out in favour of the swifter, more manoeuvrable Hughes and Bell Jet Ranger helicopters. The Hughes 500 became the workhorse of the live-capture era.

TIM AND PRUE MARRY

In 1974, Tim surprised his family and friends by marrying girlfriend Prue Hazledine at Pretoria, capital of South Africa. At the time, Tim was visiting world-famous Kruger National Park to study the live capture of wildlife. He'd invited Prue, then working in London in the film industry, to join him on holiday. On an impulse Tim proposed, Prue accepted, and they were wed at a registry office in Pretoria.

Velvet awaits processing at the Luggate factory.

That era peaked in 1979 when Alpine Helicopters caught over 7,000 wild deer. They all went to farms, including two (Criffel near Wanaka and Mararoa near Te Anau) that were owned by Tim's ever-expanding company. As well as owning 40 helicopters in his various businesses, Tim now had an interest in deer recovery, deer farming, making medicinal products from deer for Asian markets, and exporting live deer to Asia. He was a very busy man.

Many body parts of deer are processed into medicines, health tonics and other uses. Chief among these products is deer velvet. Velvet is the soft stage of antler growth. About two-thirds is water. The drying process is critical to its potency and market price. In China, dried deer velvet has been used as a medicinal product for over 2,000 years. Deer tails, sinews, pizzles, embryos and blood all have medicinal uses. In some countries, notably Korea, products made from velvet and other deer parts are thought to deliver sexual stimulation.

Other uses: deer tail hair for fine brushes and trout fishing flies; eye-teeth for jewellery; hard antler for knife handles and light brackets; and deer skin for clothing, hats, gloves and footwear.

It didn't take Tim and his Kiwi business associates very long to realise that venison was but one product of many that came from deer, and that the deer industry in New Zealand should not be afraid to get into deer-based oriental medicines and health tonics. It was a big export market.

With his Christ's College mates, Dunedin exporter Robert Wilson and Canterbury farmer Mark Acland, Tim travelled to Hong Kong and Taiwan in 1967 to

ON DEER FARMING...

'Bill Bong [Hong Kong velvet trader] put a challenge to me in 1965: Instead of killing our red deer why not farm them, just like his ancestors had done for hundred of years.'

San Francisco-based Johnny Wang grading velvet.

A small-holding of deer in Korea. Prue Wallis

explore the possibilities. The three friends shared similar interests and they had a deep respect for each other's abilities – an outstanding practical example of an 'old boys' network. Tim slotted into Asian life easily. A good host himself, he appreciated the Asian sense of hospitality.

Through expansion at his Luggate factory, Tim built an Asian export trade in deer products other than venison. He also saw an opportunity to export live deer to Asia, where the vigorous and productive red deer was an unfamiliar breed.

In 1974 Tim's company made its first airlift of 300 red deer, mostly yearlings from the Wanaka area, to Taiwan, where they were sold to farmers. The deer were trucked to Christchurch and loaded onto a stretch DC8 freighter. This consignment paved the way for live deer exports by Tim's company through the 1970s, 1980s and early 1990s to Korea, Japan, Ireland, Australia and Canada. Tim travelled to these countries many times in support of the business.

Canada was a special focus. In 1988, Tim helped create a new frontier for red deer farming in Canada through airlifts of New Zealand stock. He also became involved in a stud farm and a safari hunting business in Canada. But it wasn't all one-way traffic. In 1981, Tim's company, in association with Dunedin firm Wilson Neill Ltd, flew a consignment of Canadian elk (wapiti) to New Zealand to bolster the New Zealand red deer farm stock – the first importation of deer since 1910. It was a historic moment.

First live deer airlift – a chartered stretch DC8 loads at Christchurch for the flight to Taiwan. Prue Wallis

Tim Wallis displaying velvet at a national competition in the 1980s.

There have been many such moments in Tim's life – and lots of other moments just as important to his survival in business. One occurred in the late 1980s. Tax changes introduced by the Government threatened lots of businesses, and banks grew nervous. The Bank of New Zealand, which had lent Tim's firm large sums of money, said it wanted to inspect his operation. Three executives arrived from the Wellington head office. Tim had a programme in mind, starting with a helicopter flight in the mountains around Mt Aspiring, west of Wanaka. The executives looked happy. That sounded better than warming a seat in a Wellington tower block. Tim was in his element, shooting his visitors through tight tree-lined gorges, over icefields, glaciers and dizzying drop-offs, past cliff faces and skimming dense forest. It was all pretty stomach-churning. The bankers' faces turned pale. One man vomited.

When, after lunch, Tim suggested they fly over his deer farm, the bankers looked at their watches, mumbled something about a plane to catch out of Dunedin, and promptly declared they'd seen enough!

A major reorganisation of Tim's business interests happened in 1986 when the tourism elements were launched as a public company, The Helicopter Line. Although Tim was its largest shareholder, he was no longer the only 'boss'. And only a year after this transformation of his business, the bottom fell out of the sharemarket. The October 1987 crash, triggered by collapses on Wall Street and other major international stock exchanges, caused mayhem in the New Zealand business world. Of the 100-odd local companies formed in the previous 12 months, only five survived. The Helicopter Line was one of them.

But it was not without its casualties. They began downsizing on deer work, and some of Tim's oldest friends and employees were laid off. Having worked so hard to build up a base of expertise in his company, Tim was about as shocked by the staff redundancies as were those laid off. Still, the company had sold Mararoa Station, one of its deer farms, before the crash and probably for several million dollars more than it would have been worth a few months later.

Within a year of the crash, The Helicopter Line began buying tourism companies. Maui Campervans was first, followed by Newmans' campervan fleet and the popular Kelly Tarlton's Underwater World. The Helicopter Line went on to own Treble Cone skifield, various major tourist hotels, the Milford Track guided walk and Red Boats cruise business at Milford Sound. The company's expanding empire reached into Australia and South Africa, and there were several hundred employees in the group. Tim regularly appeared on the *National Business Review*'s 'Rich List'.

Imported Canadian elk surround Tim's vehicle at Criffel Deer Farm.

CHAPTER 6

TIM'S 'NAVY'

IT'S WELL KNOWN that Tim had an air force comprising a large fleet of helicopters, a DC-3 freighter nicknamed Stagliner, because it was used for deer transport around New Zealand, several fixed-wing light aircraft and, in later years, a collection of vintage fighter planes. Less well known is the fact he had a number of vessels — enough to say he had a 'navy'.

The largest were the *Ranginui* and *Hotunui*. They'd both been used in the coastal trade before container shipping displaced them. *Ranginui* was 32 metres long and 158 tons, a floating fridge for deer carcasses. *Hotunui*, larger at 50 metres long and 594 tons, was more like a freezer. Both went to Fiordland to act as mobile bases for the helicopter deer recovery work. They served as helipad, hotel, café, and of course cold storage space for all the deer carcasses. *Ranginui* would later receive live deer. Tim's navy included launches, too, including a jetboat called *Big Bertha*, plus an old carferry for a short time, and a wooden barge,

the *Koutinui*, nicknamed Noah's Ark.

But the *Ranginui* was the flagship. She spent four years in the Fiordland venison trade. Tim developed such a strong attachment to the little coaster he kept her based in Fiordland for holidays and hospitality for another 20-odd years. She became an adventure, a remote experience, an entertainment centre, and a fishing and hunting expedition base for wave after wave of visitors of all ages, nationalities and occupations. For most of her recreational years she was anchored at sheltered spots in Dusky or Breaksea Sounds — a long way from tarseal and television, shops and cinemas.

Tim at sea aboard the Ranginui.

Previous page: The Ranginui, *a former coastal trader, at a mooring at the head of Milford Sound, Fiordland.* Janice Wallis

You got there by helicopter. Tim had his favourite routes. On one, you flew to 'Campbell's Kingdom' – a steep-sided, curving valley of small forest-bound lakes connected by a tumbling river of white water that exited suddenly into Doubtful Sound like something out of the *Lord of the Rings* movies. You'd often see deer on the gravel lake shores. Tim also flew a more direct route via Wilmot Pass, where there is a road connecting Deep Cove (Doubtful Sound) with Lake Manapouri. Lots of tourist buses use it, and the drivers and passengers would get an awful fright when Tim 'buzzed' them. When they arrived at Breaksea Sound and at the first sight of the ship, looking tiny in this landscape, Tim would roar out, '*RAAANGINUUI!*'.

The arrival of children added a new dimension to Tim's life and to the *Ranginui* experience. He and Prue had four boys – four in five years. In age order they were: Toby, Jonathan (Jo-Jo), Matthew (Matt) and Nicholas (Nick). They had holidays at the *Ranginui* from an early age. The four little boys would be jammed into the front seats of the helicopter alongside their dad, and their mum would be in the back with the gear. Through these holidays in deepest, darkest Fiordland the boys learnt to dive, swim, fish and hunt. They messed about in small craft and water-skied behind the jet-boat. Tim couldn't go far into the bush with them because of his paralysed left leg but he could teach them how to recognise deer footprints and browse-signs in the trees.

The fiord water was a different story. Here, Tim was in his element. With scuba gear and a flipper on his good leg, he taught the boys to dive for paua and crayfish (which their father called 'beetles'). And they explored the fabulous

Tim taking part in a tug-of-war event at a Wanaka Primary School gala day.

underwater world of black coral.

The *Ranginui* hosted birthday celebrations, school holiday jaunts and business meetings. It's hard to imagine a more social and more loved vessel than her.

As they grew older, the boys became more daring. There were some dramatic moments. During one holiday at the *Ranginui*, Tim flew two of his sons – Matt, then 15, and Nick, 13 – and two of their friends to the entrance of Dagg Sound, the next fiord north from Breaksea. They wanted to dive at an unfamiliar place. The boys entered the water in pairs with wetsuits and diving gear. Tim went off in the Hughes 500 and parked on a beach on the north side of the entrance. There, he had an

Tim's family hosted a Chinese oriental medicine group led by Madam Wu in Fiordland in the 1980s. The visitors took a fishing trip in the jet-boat, Big Bertha.

afternoon nap, which was a habit of his. When he awoke, the tide had turned. It threatened to carry the boys out to sea. Things looked alarming. Nick and his friend managed to scramble ashore but Matt and his mate, upon surfacing, found themselves too far from the shore. They were caught in the outgoing current. Tim immediately flew out to help them. His plan was to manoeuvre the helicopter low enough for the boys to grab a skid and tow them back to safety. But with a swell running this was

Tim and Robert Wilson with their sons after a successful fishing and shooting expedition in the Hunter Valley. The boys are, from left, Angus Wilson, Jonathan Wallis, Toby Wallis and Ben Wilson. They are holding Canada geese and, in Robert's case, a large trout.

Good shot: Toby Wallis with his first air-gun. Toby used an eye-patch to enhance his aim.

Tim enjoying a day out with his Hughes 500 off Bauza Island, Doubtful Sound.

highly dangerous. The helicopter could cop a wave, snag its tail rotor and go under. Slowly, in tune with the rise and fall of the sea, Tim expertly pulled the two boys back to shore.

Afterwards, aboard the *Ranginui*, Tim was typically tight-lipped about the incident. All he said was: 'It's amazing what you can do when you have to.' But the boys knew it'd been an awesome feat of flying. The Dagg Sound incident joined a collection of 'Don't tell Mum' stories!

The food on the *Ranginui* was always special. Tim liked to provide a meal of crayfish on the first night, and he'd often fly off in the helicopter to known fishing spots, park the machine on rocks and go for a dive. There was always plenty of fish, shellfish and venison on board as well. Tim became famous among family and friends for a seafood soup. His chowder was usually thick enough to stand a spoon in.

Good times were abundant, down times rare. The sandflies were undoubtedly a challenge until you got used to them. Even out on a ship more than 100 metres from the shore, there'd be biting sandflies on board making a nuisance of themselves during daylight hours. Then there were the kea. These native parrots of the southern mountains, although

SUBANTARCTIC EXPEDITION

Spider crabs, which grew twice as big as crayfish, lived in abundance in coastal waters off the subantarctic Auckland Islands south of New Zealand. Tim wondered if they were worth harvesting for the North American or Asian markets. To investigate this, he arranged a trip to the cold and lonely Auckland Islands in the *Hotunui* with Robert Wilson and a Dunedin fishing company. They took a hammering in south-westerly gales. There was a helicopter in the hold in pieces, well tied down.

The *Hotunui* stayed a week at the Auckland Islands. Spider crabs were caught in wire cages – enough for a trial sample. The Hiller helicopter was assembled and Bill Black flew it over the main island while Tim took a look at another resource – wild pigs. They'd been left there to aid shipwrecked sailors in the 1800s. Like the deer in New Zealand, the pigs had caused widespread ecological damage.

Neither the crabs nor the pigs became an export industry for Tim. The crabs yielded insufficient meat; the pigs proved too hard to shoot, being protected by extensive bush and rata forest.

Still, the trip to the Auckland Islands demonstrated just how far Tim would go to access a resource.

Tim with crayfish. Prue Wallis

TIM IN THE TROPICS

Unsuitable for the Fiordland deer work, the *Hotunui* was assigned to something altogether different. She was sent to the New Hebrides (now Vanuatu), in the tropical Western Pacific, to assist a beef export business that Tim hoped to establish there.

Cattle grazing under coconut palms had become too numerous on the northern island of Espiritu Santo. New Caledonia, another tropical island group under French administration, wanted beef. The *Hotunui* would link the two, Tim reckoned. A DC-3 freighter, with a helicopter on board was also sent to the New Hebrides.

Things did not get off to a good start. The ship grounded on a reef and had to be pulled off at the next high tide. There were problems slaughtering the cattle. The workers decided themselves when to take holidays. Officialdom had two speeds, said Tim – dead slow and stop!

Hotunui *leaving Port Chalmers for the New Hebrides in support of Tim's beef export venture.*

'Gee, it's primitive here...' Tim wrote to his friend Mark Acland back home. He admitted the experience had been 'pretty depressing'.

The *Hotunui* made just four trips to New Caledonia. Within six months, Tim had decided to quit the project. When he got an offer for the ship, he sold her. That was the end of his tropical venture.

Residents of Espiritu Santo in the New Hebrides admire the newly arrived helicopter. The residents called the helicopter 'Mix-master belongum Jesus Christ.'

thought of as alpine birds, would visit the *Ranginui* out of curiosity. Kea are incredibly cheeky. On the ship they'd chew through cables, attack the hard-rubber roofing on the wheelhouse and rip holes in the helicopter seats if the doors were open.

The *Ranginui* was the last of the significant vessels in Tim's life. In May 1995, 28 years after buying her, she developed a major leak and sank at her anchorage in Breaksea Sound in 60 metres of water. In such a remote location there was really nothing that could be done to save her.

Tim was dismayed by the loss of his beloved *Ranginui*. He and others dived on her and they recovered the ship's visitor book. Even after ten days at the bottom of the fiord, the book was able to be dried out and returned to almost original condition.

It was a souvenir of a great little ship and all the people who had worked and holidayed aboard her – a ship that launched a thousand laughs and dozens of pranks. With her sinking, Tim's 'navy', already much reduced, lost its heart and soul.

ARCTIC
OCEAN

BERING
SEA

NORWAY
SWEDEN
FINLAND
• Murrnansk

• St Petersburg

BELARUS

Magadan •
Kamchatka
Peninsula

☆ Moscow

• Kursk

RUSSIA

UKRAINE

SIBERIA

Khabarovsk •

KAZAKHSTAN

• Novosibirsk

• Barnaul

Irkutsk •

Lake
Baikal

• Gorno Altaysk

Vladivostok •

UZBEKISTAN

MONGOLIA

Harbin •

NORTH
KOREA

CHINA

Feeding out hay in Siberia.

CHAPTER 7

DRAMA IN RUSSIA

DURING THE LAST few years of the *Ranginui*'s life, Tim became absorbed in an enterprise about as far away from the sea as you can get – deer farming in land-locked southern Siberia, Russia. Siberia's Gorni Altai region was not only remote from the sea; it was remote from Western business and Western ways of doing things. For a very long time it had been an unwelcoming zone for Westerners, hidden away behind Russia's Communist 'Iron Curtain'. In short, a 'no go' area.

Until 1990, Russia projected a confrontational image to much of the world. But Tim simply saw that as a challenge, something to overcome. Since the 1960s he'd known that a magnificent strain of elk deer called maral lived in southern Siberia. He wanted to go there. He was fascinated by how large these animals were compared to their red deer cousins in New Zealand. The wapiti elk from Canada were the nearest equivalents. In Russia, the maral deer produced antler velvet of phenomenal size. As his company's involvement in the velvet market

in Asia increased through the Luggate factory's output, Tim's interest in the deer of southern Siberia quickened.

He made enquiries through the 1970s and 1980s. In the end, Russia came to him. A deer farming delegation from Gorni Altai arrived in New Zealand to look at how the Kiwis were doing it. Tim's Criffel Deer Farm near Wanaka was a must-see. The Russians insisted on a reciprocal visit. Tim was only too pleased to be included in the New Zealand delegation that went to Gorni Altai in April 1989.

Today's Russia is nothing like the Russia of the 1950s to the 1980s. Those were the years of the 'Cold War' and the 'Iron Curtain'. The post-war Union of Soviet Socialist Republics (USSR) – 'Russia' for short – was a scary place. Big and scary. It was the largest country in the world, almost two and a half times the size of the United States of America. It was under strict Communist rule. Western ways of doing business were outlawed. In Russia, all you produced for export, and all imports, were channelled through government agencies in Moscow, the capital. From the outside, Russia appeared to be full of grim-faced people struggling to make a living. The military and the secret police were all-powerful. They maintained tight border controls, and relations between the USSR and America, the two 'superpowers', were cool, menacing and strained almost to the point of war – hence the term, 'Cold War'.

From the time he arrived and drank his first vodka toast, Tim was captivated by the place – the breathtaking mountains and valleys, a savagely extreme climate (as cold as minus 30°C through a prolonged winter and a sweltering 30°C in summer), and of course, the magnificent maral deer. Then there were the people, a mix of White Russian and Mongolian. This is where Asia meets Europe. The high mountains backing the region form the border for Russia, Mongolia and China. With the aid of a helicopter and plenty of cold-weather gear you could stand in three countries at once and drink a toast to all three amid the snow!

Gorni Altai had a population of 200,000 (similar to, say, the Otago region's in New Zealand). About 40,000 people lived in its main town, Gorno Altaysk. Getting there from the Russian capital, Moscow, involved a flight of four hours to the Siberian capital Novosibirsk or a smaller city south of there, then a drive of several more hours over seriously rough roads, usually at breakneck speed.

Life in this forbidden land was an eye-opener for Tim. Standouts: the lunchtime feasts featuring salami and

The 1989 New Zealand deer farming delegation to Russia at Karagai farm. Inspecting velvet with farm manager Peter Popov Junior (right) are James Guild, Bruce Gaffikin and Tom Williams.

fried potatoes; the repetitive downing of vodka with food or without it, and the backward appearance of the villages whose grocery shops were invariably poorly stocked.

Farming here was a world apart from the New Zealand experience. Livestock included camels and yaks as well as the more familiar cattle and deer. Men and women on horseback managed the stock. Working dogs were seldom seen. Under Communism, the farms – 'low tech' by New Zealand standards – were organised as collectives run by officials. Hundreds of people, sometimes

A high-altitude toast: New Zealanders Mark Acland, Mike Bringans and Tim visit the snow-bound border of Siberia, Mongolia and China, a helicopter flight from the Gorni Altai region.

thousands, worked on the larger farms. Their produce was sold and distributed through a Moscow government agency, which also controlled how much each farm received in return.

Tim was introduced to local people by another New Zealander, Bruce Gaffikin, who had worked for the New Zealand Dairy Board in Russia for many years. Through an interpreter they were able to talk to the Altai officials and farmers, who quickly warmed to Tim's personality and his obvious interest in sharing food and vodka with them. In Russia, if you didn't drink vodka you wouldn't do much business. Right from the start, Tim had a business in mind: he wanted to establish a maral deer farm, breed the best animals and sell their genetic material (fertile eggs or embryos, and semen) to other countries. He figured that kind of trade would generally benefit deer farming worldwide and, in particular, boost the Asian market for deer-velvet products.

Tim's presence in the Altai region – a Western businessman – was stunningly novel for the locals. Around this time, the USSR, under President Gorbachev, was going through a period of reform and opening up to the world at large. Tim and his colleague, Bruce Gaffikin, were the first Westerners to make an impression in the Altai region. They came with plenty of ideas on how to lift the economy and the wealth of the region. But Tim's prime objective was to develop a deer genetics export business.

First, he got the region's political leaders on side. There were meetings, dinners, vodka, and trips to see his operation in New Zealand. He looked around for land to lease for a stud farm. It didn't look easy but Tim pressed on, determined as ever.

He was so taken by the Altai and its people he thought his wife, Prue, and their four sons – Toby, Jonathan,

CASH IN CALLIPER

Tim always carried a wad of American dollars when travelling in Russia. It paid to have cash in hand because of Russia's inflation rate, an uncertain banking system, and the influence you could have flashing around American currency. He'd hide the cash in the steel calliper that supported his left leg. One time, while visiting a remote village accessible only by riverboat with the head of the Polikarpov restoration project, he lost a money belt bulging with American cash from his room at the guest lodge. Police were called, the robber was caught and Tim got back all but $3,000 of the stolen money. It turned out that the boyfriend of the receptionist gave the thief a key to the important-looking foreigner's room. He hoped the stolen money went to worthy causes in the village.

Matthew and Nick – should also see the region. At the start of the August school holidays in 1991, when the boys ranged in age from 15 to 11, the family left their Wanaka home with snow on the surrounding mountains for a summery Siberia. They'd heard about the political tension building in Moscow – President Gorbachev's reformers versus the hard-line Communists – but were not concerned about their safety.

In the Altai, the Wallises were treated as special guests of the regional government. Tim expected the boys to behave accordingly, especially at banquets. If their body language suggested displeasure with the food, he'd give them looks

Sir Peter Elworthy (left) and Tim enjoy lunch at a deer farm.

Prue and the boys went horse-trekking at Karagai farm.

that said: 'You will eat this – and enjoy it!' Privately, they thought the region's shops, vehicles and roads looked tatty and behind the times. But they loved the adventurous side of life.

The highlight was a five-day rafting trip on the Kartun River. It wasn't exactly adventure tourism as New Zealand knew it. Their father had arranged the whole thing. The guides were dairy factory workers co-opted for the trip and the rafts were fashioned from deflated rubber pontoons on the river bank. To pump them up, the guides took a length of hose, slipped one end over the exhaust pipe of a Lada van and the other into the pontoon opening, and revved the Lada's engine like mad. Next, the inflated pontoons were bound together by poles freshly cut from birch trees, and a piece of cargo netting was slung between the poles to carry the gear and food for camping. The paddles were home made.

The Kartun River was swift and in the gorges it turned into bucking waves

Tim and Nick rafting the Kartun River.

of white water. Seeing no people until the last day, the family and their escorts camped on quiet river banks and ate boiled beef, cucumbers, tomatoes, cheese and bread. Tim, preoccupied by deer farm visits, choppered in on the last day, bringing with him a pig that broke the boredom of the meals.

The boys also enjoyed horse-trekking on Karagai farm, the region's finest deer farm, where their father had been negotiating to buy stock. The horses were used to rough going despite being unshod. Toby, the oldest boy, was thrown off his mount when it bolted with him holding a video camera in one hand and the reins in the other. When the trek into the hill country got going, it became a magical experience. The boys saw hundreds of elk cows and calves grazing the flower-filled meadows between patches of forest, and later they gathered alpine berries and pine nuts, guided by the sons of farm workers.

At the end of the three-week holiday the family travelled to Moscow to head home. They landed right in the middle of a revolutionary episode in Russian history. There had been riots in Red Square. Tanks had charged a crowd, killing several people. The Wallises saw the aftermath – flower posies on the kerbside and barricades around the Parliament. Tim and Prue felt that as they were not part of the upheaval they'd be safe. And they were.

By the end of that year the USSR ceased to exist. To the astonishment of the rest of the world, it disintegrated into independent republics. Russia, the largest of them, began opening itself up to world trade, market forces and Western business interests. Tim and Bruce Gaffikin, forming a company called Altyn Kerl, tried a few ventures but Tim's real mission here was in maral deer genetics. Despite political support, officialdom continued to frustrate his plans for a stud farm. Even more obstinate were the farm directors and managers whom he relied on for stock and support. They were staunch: there'd be no exporting of maral genetics, which they regarded as theirs to profit from in the new economic era.

Tim engaged a New Zealand farmer to manage the project but progress remained painfully slow. Some fencing was installed on a leased farm, deer yards were erected, and a plant and machinery acquired.

Tim talking to curious Russian children after arriving at their farm village in the Altai region in a Mil 6 helicopter.

ON WORKING IN RUSSIA . . .

'It's unbelievably hard.'

'When I was in dangerous situations I'd make sure I was well looked after.'

Tim, accompanied by Manuel, inspects wartime aircraft wrecks in the disputed Kuril Islands between Japan and Russia's Kamchatka Peninsula. Alpine Fighter Collection

Opposite: Engine tests prior to the maiden flight of Tim's first Polikarpov I-16. Alpine Fighter Collection

Meanwhile, dark forces were operating. Since the unleashing of a free market, white-collar gangs, known as the 'Russian mafia', were expanding. People at the edge of Tim's business dealings were turning up dead. For some years Tim had had the assistance of two reliable local men, Manuel and Armin, for transport (mainly car or helicopter) in the Altai region and for arranging meetings. Manuel kept a semi-automatic pistol handy, and he was an expert in using gifts of beer and cigarettes to secure a favour. In Russia, bribery was commonplace.

With business interests always on the go at home, Tim travelled to Altai for weeks at a time. By 1994, after more frustration with officials and word of more mafia mischief, he decided enough was enough. He loathed wasting time and resources. Tim pulled the plug on his Russian deer genetics dream and abandoned everything without warning. Everything to do with the deer genetics and farming, that is.

There was one other element to his Russian operation however – vintage fighter aircraft. Through the early 1990s he had been collecting the wrecks of planes downed in the Second World War in the tundra and other remote places in Russia. His main focus had been a Russian fighter, the Polikarpov. An aircraft factory in the Siberian capital, Novosibirsk, restored several of these old planes in a unique project set up by Tim and his Wanaka-based company Alpine Deer Group. It was the first time any of these planes had been restored.

Thankfully, there was no mafia influence in this industry so, although it was slow and expensive, the project was a success.

The first of Alpine's Polikarpovs had its maiden flight in 1995 and the others followed at intervals over a four-year period – nine altogether. They were delivered in wooden crates to Wanaka Airport, the venue for one of Tim's most striking achievements – Warbirds Over Wanaka.

CHAPTER 8

WARBIRDS

'LOOK RIGHT!' says the voice over the public address system. Forty thousand heads do just that. Unlike the commentator, who is perched on the top deck of a red double-decker bus, the spectators are at ground level. They don't exactly know what to expect or from which direction the action will come. Will it be a sleek Spitfire chasing the gutsy gull-winged Vought Corsair? Will it be the other way around? Either way, they know they're about to see piston-engined warplanes going at somewhere near peak performance on a low-level swoop the length of the runway – close enough and fast enough to make it a neck-wrenching experience for the crowd.

Another Warbirds Over Wanaka has begun. Every second Easter since 1988, WOW has put on two days of aerial displays by aircraft old and new – 10 am to 4 pm. Non-stop. Not even a lunch break. From all over the country and from overseas as well, people descend on Wanaka Airport in their thousands, jamming the adjacent highway with cars and campervans. They're pleased to see the air force's latest planes and other snappy new creations but really they've come to admire and salute the vintage stuff, especially the fighter aircraft of the Second World War. Spitfire, Mustang, Corsair, Kittyhawk, Hurricane, Lavochkin, Polikarpov, Messerschmitt, Zero and so on.

It's the biggest airshow of its kind in New Zealand or Australia. And it's right up there on a world scale, too. The spectators are close to the action, close enough to feel the blasts and heat from the pyrotechnics and fireballs that simulate wartime battle as the fighter planes flash overhead.

Tim dreamed up the concept in the early 1980s. Having flown a number of fixed-wing aircraft over the years, he decided he'd like to own a fighter plane of Second World War vintage. Perhaps more than one. They weren't cheap but he had the money. His achievements in deer recovery, deer farming and the world of helicopters had paid off. He was a millionaire. His first purchase, in 1984, was an American fighter, a P-51D Mustang, which he displayed at the Royal New Zealand Air Force 'Wings and Wheels' pageant at Wigram airfield in January the following year.

Asked by a newspaper reporter why he had acquired it, Tim replied: 'I bought it for its historic value. It's a shame there are not more of these planes around.'

Tim, Prue and the boys with John Dilley, the Mustang's previous owner.

An impressive line-up: four I-16 Polikarpovs over the mountains around Wanaka. Phil Makanna

Although Tim valued these old planes for the role they played in the Second World War, he was just as interested in their design – simple by today's standards – and their stunningly fast and efficient performance. While at Christ's College in the early 1950s he had seen Wigram-based Mustangs and other warplanes zoom across the city at full throttle at fairly low level. He remembered biking out to Wigram occasionally in the hope of a closer look at them.

Now he had one himself. But that was just the start.

By 1987, Tim was planning a whole airshow. He contacted the Auckland-based New Zealand Warbirds Association, which said it would be glad to

Prue and four-year-old Nick Wallis in the first Mustang, 1984.

contribute vintage planes, and he involved his brother, George, who was a collector of vintage vehicles and machinery. The idea was to make the airshow something of a country fair, with machinery and other displays, including re-created Second World War military scenarios. Over Easter 1988, with the assistance of a few enthusiasts, including Wanaka Lions Club members, the Wallis brothers presented Warbirds On Parade at Wanaka Airport – the quiet little airfield near Luggate, where Tim had flown to with his first helicopter in 1965.

In 1988, the airfield was still pretty much an aviation backwater. The main buildings there then were those of the Alpine Deer Group and Aspiring Air.

Tim and George wondered how many people would turn up for Warbirds On Parade. An estimated 14,000 did – and they loved it. There were displays by a 1953 Hawker Sea Fury and a de Havilland Venom jet fighter as well as Tim's Mustang. The RNZAF contributed its Red Checkers aerobatic team, a Strikemaster, Iroquois helicopter and Friendship transport plane.

Warbirds had to benefit the local community as far as Tim was concerned, and some of the proceeds of the 1988 show went towards a new swimming pool for Wanaka. What next? Fired up by the turnout for the first show, Tim and George engaged a Wanaka man, Gavin Johnston, to help them manage the 1990 event. To better 'brand' it, there was a name change. It became Warbirds Over Wanaka.

Meanwhile, Tim sold the Mustang in October 1988 and two months later bought a Spitfire, the most famous British fighter type of all. This Supermarine Spitfire Mk XVI (Mark 16), registered TB863, was built in 1944, the year before the war ended. It had minor roles subsequently in two war films – *Reach for the Sky* (1955) and *Battle of Britain* (1967). The earlier film portrayed the life and flying feats of wartime pilot Douglas Bader, a double amputee who flew with tin legs and had numerous crashes.

Tim, once described as 'New Zealand's Douglas Bader' by a television documentary, had to get a special licence to fly the Spitfire. He achieved this at Auckland with the help of a New Zealand warbirds pilot, Keith Skilling.

Tim wanted to make the most of it as he delivered the Spitfire to its new home at Wanaka. In January 1989, before leaving the Auckland area, he flew his Spitfire at

an airshow at Ardmore Aiport. He then headed for Rotorua and Gisborne to put the plane through its paces. Next call was to be Masterton.

But on the way there, over southern Hawkes Bay, he had fuel problems and was forced to land in a paddock near Waipukurau. The undercarriage collapsed and the propeller was wrecked. It was embarrassing. But the Spitfire wasn't a write-off and was back in the air for the Easter 1990 Warbirds show. For the 28,000 spectators that year the Spitfire was a sensation as it swept low over the airfield and climbed steeply, its engine seeming to purr with the enjoyment of combining speed and aerobatic grace.

By the 1992 show, Tim was well and truly bitten by the Warbirds 'bug'. He'd become a collector of vintage fighters of different types and nationalities. He had the Spitfire, and the Polikarpov project was under way in Russia. He had an eye on other acquisitions, too.

His business associates read the signs in him: Tim was on a mission. He could afford it.

Between the Mustang and Spitfire purchases, there was a major rearrangement of his business affairs. Deer recovery and deer farming were separated from his tourism interests.

To fund warplane purchases, Tim would sometimes sell a parcel of shares. Of course, the planes were investments in their own right.

Owning these planes was only a part of the mission. Tim also wanted to have them on public display as often as possible. And he wanted to acknowledge the

Above: Forced landing at Waipukurau, January 1989.

Right: Cartoonist Tom Scott's view of the Waipukurau forced landing.
Tom Scott

YOU GOTTA HAND IT TO HIM—A ONE-LEGGED DEER FARMER FROM WANAKA HAS MANAGED TO DO WHAT THE COMBINED MIGHT OF THE 3RD REICH COULDN'T—HE DOWNED THIS SPITFIRE...

Tom Scott

contribution of the New Zealand pilots and ground crew to the war effort. An uncle of his, Neil Blunden, had been a Royal Air Force bomber pilot and died on a raid against a German battleship in Norway.

Fighter types used by the RNZAF in the Pacific during the Second World War featured in the 1992 Warbirds show – Kittyhawk and Vought Corsair. A Pacific theme carried on into the 1994 event with appearances by the Corsair and a Japanese Mitsubishi Zero replica. There were no fewer than eleven aircraft types new to the show that year. They included a torpedo-carrying Gruman Avenger, a Catalina flying boat and a plane that made Tim's heart race a little bit faster – a Spitfire Mk XIV (Mark 14). It had

Tim Wallis flying his Spitfire Mk XVI at the Warbirds Over Wanaka 1994 airshow.
Phil Makanna

been purchased for the Alpine Fighter Collection after restoration in England.

This was the year when pyrotechnics made a big impact. There was a re-enactment of the sinking of the Imperial Japanese battleship *Yamato*, represented by a canvas profile on the far side of the runway. Simulated strafing and bombing of it by the Corsair, Kittyhawk and Avenger was accompanied by deafening explosions and the eruption of fireballs wrapped in black smoke, until finally the great battleship sank from sight.

TRIBUTE TO FIGHTER PILOTS

Of the 5,000 New Zealand pilots who served in the Second World War, more than two-thirds were with the Royal Air Force in Europe. Hundreds of New Zealand pilots also served in the Pacific during that war, combating the invading Japanese forces. As a tribute to them, and the pilots of the First World War, Tim set up a New Zealand Fighter Pilots' Museum at Wanaka Airport. 'It does not seek to glorify war,' he stated at its opening in April 1993. 'The aim of the museum is to collect, preserve and display information and memorabilia relating to those who flew fighter aircraft in our defence during the First and Second World Wars.'

The Kittyhawk is chased by the Corsair. Glenn Alderton

A line-up of campervans on the terrace overlooking the airport. Chris Hinch

Tim liked the idea of incorporating stunts and special acts in Warbirds Over Wanaka. It had always been in his nature to try new or spectacular things. At the 1994 show there was a race down the runway involving a John Britten motorcycle, a helicopter and a Pitts Special biplane. The motorcycle won easily, astonishing the crowd with its acceleration.

WOW has always included helicop-ters performing to their limits with spinning dives, crazy angles and graceful pirouettes down the runway with rotor tips a metre off the seal.

Tim loved performing these stunts himself. Helicopters would sometimes show off their ability to lift an old car or caravan, and drop it from a height calculated to smash the object to bits.

Tim also liked to inject humour into

the airshows. For example, at one show the commentary team faked an interview with an American Stealth bomber pilot. The crowd was led to believe the high-tech, low-flying bomber was on its way to Wanaka. Just as the mysterious but still invisible aircraft was about to appear over the airfield, the pyrotechnics crew detonated a bone-rattling explosion around an old army tank on the opposite side of the runway from the crowd. The tank disintegrated. The Stealth bomber, stealthier than anyone anticipated, then disappeared off the airwaves. Mission accomplished. For months afterwards people in the crowd who thought they'd somehow missed sighting the cunning aircraft, wrote to the Warbirds organisers asking for a photograph of it!

The 1994 show introduced the two-day format for displays – Easter Saturday and Sunday. Later in the year Tim got to fly the Mark 14 Spitfire for the first time. He compared the plane to 'a wild gypsy woman'. By that he meant that it was more powerful and faster than a Mark 16, and that it behaved in an eccentric way. Its massive 2,000-horsepower engine spun the five-blade propeller anticlockwise (viewed from the cockpit),

Tim puts his Hughes 500 through its paces at Treble Cone, a ski field near Wanaka, for guests of the museum opening.

which required the pilot to set the rudder a certain way before take off to avoid the plane veering to the right. Airborne and going flat out, it could reach speeds of around 800 kph. Cruising, it would do 520 kph. A magnificent aircraft all round. But pilot Ray Hanna, a legend in Warbirds circles, warned Tim the Mark 14 could also be a 'beast'.

Tim's aircraft of choice remained the Mark 16. He clocked up lots of hours in it. Most of all, he loved showing off its paces to people. And not only at the airshows. He once decided to put on an

ON THE NZ FIGHTER PILOTS' MUSEUM . . .

'Preserving history is so important.'

Sir Tim and Lady Wallis beside Tim's Tigermoth at Wanaka following the announcement of Tim's knighthood.
Southland Times

SIR TIM

In May 1994, Tim became Sir Tim. He was knighted for his inspirational contribution to deer recovery aviation and deer farming, his founding of Warbirds Over Wanaka, and his support for the Burwood Spinal Injuries Unit and numerous community organisations. The knighthood, he said, was also a tribute to the people who supported him. 'Everybody will still call me Tim,' he told the *Otago Daily Times*. 'My mother will still call me Timothy. I don't think the "Sir" bit will get used very often.'

aerobatics display for spinal unit patients at Burwood Hospital in Christchurch. Tim much admired the work of the spinal unit, having been an outpatient for a long time after the 1968 crash broke his back. The Spitfire display for Burwood patients was his way of showing how someone partially paralysed could sometimes do things beyond their wildest dreams.

Tim often quoted American John Wooden: 'No one should let what they cannot do interfere with what they can do.'

So Tim advised the Burwood office that day he was coming over in the Mark 16 and would they care to tell the patients and staff to be out on the lawns. For about five minutes he performed loops, barrel rolls, Cubans, the works. The display went down well with the patients but a local resident complained of the noise and 'dangerous' manoeuvres overhead. Tim faced a court charge. The judge dismissed it, though, declaring there was 'no reason at all to enter a conviction.'

Always energetic, always seeming to be pushing limits, Tim was renowned for being fearless in the air. He had numerous mishaps in helicopters, although none fatal for his passengers. He was well known for winging it in all kinds of weather.

In the winter of 1995, he flew out of Wanaka with his second son, Jonathan, then 18, to attend a Dunedin reunion of Christ's College old boys (all four sons attended Christ's, following the family tradition). They left after lunch in Tim's Hughes 500 helicopter. Approaching the Lammermoor Range inland from Dunedin, they hit a snow storm. In white-out conditions, Tim was forced to land. But he knew they would soon be over the mountains and probably out of the snow. He asked Jonathan to walk ahead through the snow-covered clumps of tussock grass to guide him through the white-out. Jonathan tried but made little progress and soon climbed back

Two Mustangs keep clear of a fireball. Glenn Alderton

on board the grounded chopper. It soon became dark and intensely cold. Tim phoned home, saying cheerfully that they'd landed by a hut where there was food and a fire. In fact, they had only some barley sugar sweets and aged chocolate on board, and the aluminium-foil survival bags provided little comfort.

In the morning, they were still in a blizzard. But blue sky appeared faintly through the blowing snow. Jonathan cleared snow from the engine's air intake with his bare hands, a painfully cold task, and Tim fired up the helicopter. Soon they were above the blizzard. 'What a beautiful day!' he said – and that was about all – as they backtracked for home, where Prue, not fooled by the story of a hut, food and fire, had hot baths ready for them.

Towards the end of 1995, Tim's life grew more hectic than ever and seemingly more troublesome. He'd just lost his beloved *Ranginui* – sunk at her Fiordland mooring. He'd written off his Russian deer farming investments. And his shares in the big tourism company, The Helicopter Line, were dropping in value. His Alpine Deer Group directors cautioned him to slow down on the vintage warplane projects. On the positive side, he had just acquired Minaret Station, a 20,000 ha high-country farm on the Southern Alps side of Lake Wanaka, to complement the other Wanaka investments, mainly Criffel Deer Farm and the Luggate deer products factory. In Canada, he and New Zealand veterinarian Mike Bringans had teamed up to develop an elk genetics business that looked very promising. There was an awful lot on Tim's mind as Christmas approached.

CHAPTER 9

SURVIVAL

TOWARDS EVENING on New Year's Day 1996, Tim took off in his Spitfire FUP, the Mark 16, for Manapouri, an awesome mountain-lake environment at the edge of Fiordland National Park. He had a date there with several hundred scouts who were camping at an Asia-Pacific jamboree. But they didn't know he was coming. Out of a sky that carried rain clouds and an occasional rainbow, Tim made a dramatic entrance in the Spitfire, flying at full speed into a series of loops and rolls and low-level passes. The scouts were enthralled. Most of them had never seen anything like it.

And just as suddenly as he'd arrived, the Spitfire was gone, back to Wanaka before nightfall. Tim liked supporting the Scouting movement. His sons had been cubs and scouts in their boyhood.

The next day, 2 January, a Tuesday, Tim was up early as usual. He had another appointment in the air. This time it was with a pilot friend of his, Brian Hore, who co-owned a North American Mustang with Tim's Alpine company. They'd agreed to practice together for the next Warbirds airshow

three months away.

Tim had decided to fly the Mark 14 Spitfire rather than the Mark 16. That surprised Brian. He wondered if Tim had chosen the Mark 14 because it would better match the extreme speed of the Mustang. Brian was much more used to seeing Tim in the Mark 16, in which he'd clocked up about 200 hours' flying. In the Mark 14, Tim had done only five and a half hours, and it was eight months since he'd flown it.

In the cockpit of the Mark 14, Tim

Tim sitting in the cockpit of his Spitfire Mk XIV. Ian Brodie

Opposite: Wreckage of the Spitfire Mk XIV, with the propeller gouge mark in the foreground and left wing in the air.

went through pre-flight checks while Brian readied the Mustang for take off. Then Tim struck a problem and shut down the engine. The radio wasn't working. While a colleague of Tim's looked at the faulty radio, Brian flew the Mustang out over Lake Wanaka and waited.

At the Fighter Pilots' Museum, Ian Brodie was busy organising a busload of Australian visitors when Tim took out the Spitfire. Ian opened the door so the visitors could get a good look at the Spitfire taking off.

With the radio working again, Tim fastened his flying helmet, a Second World War leather type, and gunned the Spitfire's powerful Rolls Royce Griffon engine. It accelerated swiftly. Then, just airborne and about halfway along the runway – and to the horror of the onlookers – it began veering to the right.

Too late, Tim realised what was wrong: he'd failed to manually preset the rudder trim fully left during the pre-flight checks. In a hurry to get airborne ... distracted by the glitch with the radio ... and with a hundred-and-one business things on his mind at the end of a frustrating year, he'd overlooked the full-left rudder setting. You didn't need that kind of setting on the Mark 16, which he'd flown the day before. For take off in the Mark 14, though, with its additional 600 horsepower and the propeller turning in the opposite direction, it was critical.

Tim tried frantically to counter the plane's swerve to the right. But he needed space to correct his mistake. Too soon he came upon the airport boundary fence. The plane's tail wheel snagged the top two wires. With a jerk, its nose lifted. Then the aircraft stalled. Falling to its right, it struck the flat paddock on the airport margins about 130 metres from the fenceline. On contact with the ground, the right wing snapped off at its base. The plane continued rolling right, upside down now, with the propeller's wooden blades gouging a trench and sheering off after a short distance.

The wrecked Spitfire came to rest 170 metres from the breach in the fence. Wire was still entangled in the tail wheel. Underneath the wreck, upside down and still harnessed in the shattered cockpit, Tim lay unconscious and unmoving.

Ian Brodie was out of the museum like a shot. He and airport colleagues

The demolished canopy and cockpit of Tim's Spitfire Mk XIV.

Grant Bisset and Jeff McHaffie were first on the scene. The ground was awash with aviation fuel, which was still hosing out of ruptured tanks. Engine oil was also spewing out and smoking as it contacted hot metal. The engine had stopped but was crackling as it cooled.

The wreck was a potential firebomb. Foam from fire extinguishers was quickly spread over the ground, the plane and cockpit area.

At first, the rescuers thought Tim was dead. Then they heard a gurgle. There was also a small movement. More people arrived, including Tim's oldest son, Toby, aged 20, who was flying for Wanaka-based Biplane Adventures at the time and in the process of getting his commercial helicopter licence.

The plane had to be turned to get Tim out. Everyone pitched in to lift the intact left wing until it was pointing into the air. Was Tim still alive? Could they safely remove him? The left side of his face was shockingly ripped and cut. He had fearful head injuries.

Releasing Tim from his safety harness and parachute strap, the rescuers eased him out – no mean feat given Tim's weight and bulk and the mangled condition of the cockpit. Tim was still gurgling. Barrie McHaffie, of Aspiring Air, cleared Tim's mouth of soil, blood and vomit to try to restore his breathing. He was placed in the 'recovery' position to await emergency services.

Ian Brodie's next thoughts were for Prue. Someone had to go and tell her. He drove down Mt Barker Road from the airport with the gravel and dust flying.

At Benfiddich, Prue was in the kitchen when Ian burst in. He told her Tim had had an accident. Thinking he might have crashed during aerobatics practice, Prue asked, 'Did he fall out of the sky?' No, Ian explained, the accident had happened at take off. 'Is he alive?' asked Prue. Ian was noncommittal. The best he could say was that Tim was unconscious.

'He'll be all right then,' said Prue.

Ambulance, doctor and fire appliances arrived but what Tim needed urgently was a transfer by air to Dunedin Hospital's intensive care unit. By the time an Air Aspiring Britten-Norman Islander plane took off with him, Prue had arrived at the crash scene, as had his youngest son, Nick. Nick, 15, was on holiday from Christ's College and had hoped his father would fly him and some friends to Minaret Station that day. When Nick saw his father stretched out in the paddock he didn't recognise him. His face was too disfigured.

Third son, Matthew, turning 17 the next day, was driving back from a holiday in Canterbury and second son Jonathan was in England. Jonathan's mum phoned him later in the day, having arranged a flight home for him. She said Tim had been involved in a Spitfire crash. He had a 'bang on his head'.

Tim arrived at the hospital still unconscious – condition 'critical'. That night he was operated on for over six hours. The skin on the left side of his face had been stripped. He had fractures to his left eye orbit and cheek bones. The biggest concern was the battering the left front side of his brain took. The associated swelling could kill him. The next few days would determine whether he lived or died.

Hospital consultants prepared the family for the worst. First, he'd be lucky to live through so horrendous a head injury. In their opinion, he had less than a ten percent chance of even regaining consciousness. Forget about his getting back to anything like a normal life.

Prue had another view, though. He'd recover. He'd do much better than predicted. He was only 57 years old. What did the medical staff know about Tim's determination? Or hers, for that matter?

The intensive care continued, with Tim surrounded by lines, wires and tubes. Prue and the boys were constantly at his side. They spoke or read to him as normal, hoping Tim would hear even while in a coma and be encouraged to fight back to consciousness. They held up photos to his unseeing eyes. The nurses also kept up a one-way conversation while taking care of dressings, washing or moving him.

After two and a half weeks, still in a coma, Tim was transferred to a neuro-surgical ward. He'd survived the initial trauma.

To challenge Tim's sense of hearing, the Wallises introduced taped sounds that were a strong part of Tim's life – a fired-up Spitfire engine, for example. Alpine Deer Group colleagues gave updates on business things as if Tim were sitting up and taking notice. The family's Jack Russell dog, Digger, was brought along to meet Tim again. But no one could say when he would wake up. A head injury this severe was unpredictable.

Sharon Mackie (left) and physiotherapist Lyn Weedon helping Tim to walk. Prue Wallis

Prue began talking of treating Tim at home. 'Way too early,' said the specialists. But she persisted. What would Tim, an outdoors man, think of being cooped up in a room smaller than a prison cell? He needed intensive nursing and specialist equipment, no question. But couldn't this be replicated at home? Prue started making arrangements. First, she appointed an intensive care nurse, Michael Lucas, to head a home-based team.

Then, as if on cue, Tim began to respond. At the end of his seventh week in hospital, Prue asked him, without expecting a reply, if he wanted to see some photos of fencing work at Minaret Station. Tim was in a Lazyboy chair, eyes closed as usual. To Prue's astonishment, he suddenly mumbled something like: 'See ... Minaret photos.' The consultant, Albert Erasmus, was called.

'This is Dr Erasmus,' said Prue. 'The boys call him Dr Razzmatazz.'

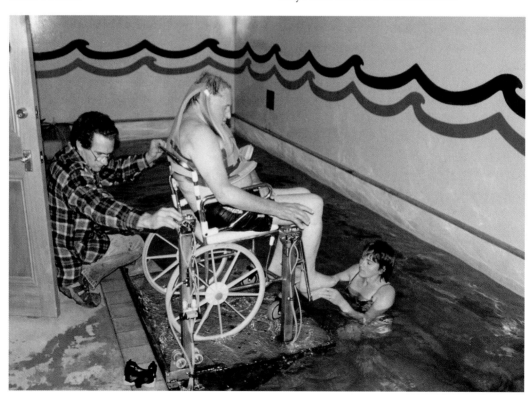

Slowly, Tim extended a hand. In a slurred voice he said, 'How do you do… Razzmatazz.'

The consultant laughed. He said he'd often had patients wake up angry, confused and violent but none had ever shaken hands with him coming out of a coma.

That evening Tim said, 'Hello Prue.' He also named the boys. Anything he said, no matter how mumbled, was music to the ears of his family. These first words after the crash intensified plans for his return home.

On 26 February, eight weeks after the crash, Tim went home to Wanaka semi-conscious and utterly dependent on round-the-clock nursing. He was unable to sit up or swallow. He couldn't speak or see clearly, and couldn't remember what he'd said. He slept about 20 hours a day. He had a special tilting bed at home, and all the medical gear needed to support him. The family were sure he would respond more quickly in the familiar surroundings of his home, Benfiddich (Deer Mountain), amidst the dry summer air of the Upper Clutha Valley, the autumn mating calls of the deer, and the treasured memorabilia of home. These personal treasures included

. . . .
ON THE 1996 CRASH…

'Survival, I am sure, is a combination of good reactions and a factor we will name Lady Luck… If I had been in this accident in the war I would not have recovered.'

'I do not remember anything… I can only remember arriving back home in Wanaka and wondering why I had so much equipment around me.'

Opposite: Alpine Fighter Collection engineer Malcolm Brown adjusting the hydraulic platform that lowers Tim into the pool at his home in Wanaka. Physiotherapist Lyn Weedon is in the pool. Prue Wallis

a collection of ornamental turtles, given to Tim over the years by friends who knew how many crashes he'd survived – and who called him 'Turtle'. Tim, they all knew, had a very hard shell.

Gradually, he became more awake and responsive. A rehabilitation team took up the challenge – physiotherapist, occupational therapist, and nurses skilled in treating people with a brain injury. The therapists briefed family members and business associates on how they could help, how they needed to not just give passive support to Tim but to actively participate in his 'rehab'.

In the second week of March, Tim had his first outing in a car – to see his brother, George, who lived not far from Benfiddich and was having a birthday. Tim was floppy and could hardly speak but he managed a garbled 'Happy birthday, George'.

Easter and the 1996 Warbirds Over Wanaka brought a new challenge. On the eve of the airshow, some of the pilots flew over Benfiddich, waggling wings in salute. Tim was wheeled out, propped up, and watched with one good eye. He could hear the planes roaring past.

For the show itself he used a special wheelchair and watched from a small

Nurse Sharon Mackie and the four Wallis boys take Tim snorkelling at the Vatulele Island Resort in Fiji. Prue Wallis

marquee on the terrace above the airfield. He saw the rare German ME-109 fighter perform, and a Russian Yak-3 emblazoned with red stars. Tim's Mark 16 Spitfire was flown by his friend, veteran pilot Ray Hanna. Tim recorded a few words for the show's organisers and pilots. He spoke like someone severely affected by a stroke. Many listening to him couldn't make out what he was saying.

Yet Tim was on the mend. On Easter Monday he sat up unaided for the first time. Had the Warbirds show worked some magic on him?

The physio and occupational therapists responded to his 'will to fight', now clearly visible. Physical challenges were stepped up and goals set: sitting, standing, walking and talking clearly.

As soon as he was well enough to be driven on a regular basis, he went back to his desk at the Alpine Deer Group office at Wanaka Airport. Here, he was surrounded by stimulating memorabilia – model planes, antlers, deer skins, a Russian pilot's helmet, framed certificates, dramatic photographs – and ornamental turtles. The 'office work' included physio and massage sessions.

The weather cut up rough at Bells Hut, Minaret Station, when Tim made one of his first flights into the mountains following his Spitfire crash. The day started out fine enough for a barbecue for Tim's rehabilitation and medical team, but suddenly turned to rain. Prue Wallis

He tired quickly. A room out the back became 'Tim's Flat', where he rested and slept surrounded by files, films and photos recording his past achievements.

From the start of the rehabilitation, Tim clearly wanted to give his all to every task the therapists set. But he had to go right back to basics. Learn from scratch. He even had to learn to write again, as his eyesight (he had little sight in his left eye as a result of the crash) and eye-hand coordination were severely impaired. He needed guidance on how to use a pen. Occupational therapy is all about this sort of thing. OT Mariann Fairbairn, who had worked with brain-injured people before, looked at films, photos and other records of Tim's activities before the crash. From these she developed signposts for triggering his memory.

Routines were hugely important. So were rest periods. He began recalling events and people from the past that his office staff had all but forgotten. He got back into the pool at home and, slowly, awkwardly, began swimming again. By September – nine months after the crash – he was able to complete ten lengths of the eleven metre pool using a snorkel. He was also now taking his first steps with the aid of a walking frame.

He went flying again in a dual-control helicopter. His support people doubted whether he would get his pilot's licence back but the flying would at least offer another rung on the ladder of recovery. He'd already confounded the specialists' predictions. Not only had he survived; he was getting out and about. Who could say how far the rehab would take him? People began talking about the 'Tim Wallis factor'.

Brain injury often affects the victim's personality. Tim lost his characteristic

A PUBLIC OUTPOURING

The Spitfire crash and Tim's critical condition made headline news around New Zealand and in countries such as Britain, the United States, Russia, Japan and Germany. Dunedin Hospital was deluged with flowers and 'Get well' cards and letters. Over the first couple of months Tim and the family received 3,000 items of mail.

One enormous card contained over 700 signatures. It was sent from the international scout camp near Manapouri. Another card came from admirers in North America. There were 200 signatures underneath a message addressed to Tim: 'We know you don't mind these plane crashes, but we are stressing out over it!'

When Tim could write again, he set about replying personally to all the well-wishers.

Proud moment: Nick Wallis is congratulated by his dad and brothers Matthew and Jonathan on his success rowing for Christ's College in an interschool championship at Lake Ruataniwha, South Canterbury, in March 1998. Prue Wallis

smile during the three months in hospital. But back at Benfiddich it returned. By the end of 1996, his sense of humour was returning. So was his courteous and generous nature. All this was a relief to family and friends who worried he might become a stranger – a highly dependent stranger – in their midst.

A national magazine, *North and South*, carried Tim's story in its November 1996 edition. On the cover was a picture of him with his Fox Moth biplane at Wanaka Airport. The story was titled, 'Never Say Die'. Writer Cate Brett said Tim had beaten the odds again. Two

years earlier she'd written another major article about Tim for the same magazine, describing Tim's knack of surviving adversities in the air, the business world and in life generally.

'This accident has brought me to heel,' Tim told Cate Brett at the time. 'It has taught me to appreciate my wife and my sons and my friends. I have always loved them but now I am telling them I love them. I want my sons to know how important they are to me.'

The youngest sons, Matthew and Nick, still at Christ's College, had spent the first term of 1996 at Wanaka's Mt Aspiring College so they could be near their dad. Matthew spoke for all four boys when he said it was a joy to have their father at home instead of his always being away on business trips.

'Yes, I'm damaged,' Tim told Cate Brett. 'But I'm not buggered.'

CHAPTER 10

TIM'S WAY

TIM'S MIDDLE NAME is William. It could just as easily be Willpower. Without it – without determination, persistence and enthusiasm to burn – Tim could never have achieved any sort of recovery from the Spitfire crash. It's tempting to call his 'rehab' a miracle. A lot of people think it is. But really, it's all about grittiness. Tim has pushed limits all his life and he wasn't about to let a brain injury immobilise him or stop him working on new ideas.

As the Warbirds shows rolled around, he wanted to be in the thick of the organising. The 1998 show had a Russian theme – 'Red Stars Rising'. Its stars were the Polikarpov fighters from the Alpine collection and the Siberian project that restored them. There were five in the air at once. No one had seen as many planes of this type flying in formation in over 50 years, not even in Russia.

Warbirds 2000 was another special moment for Tim. A Hawker Hurricane fighter, cousin of the more famous Spitfire, made its first appearance. Tim had recovered well enough to be able

Buzz Aldrin acknowledges the crowd on a drive-by with Tim and Warbirds general manager Gavin Johnston. Mike Jorgensen

Tim flying in the Southern Alps in 1994. Phil Makanna

ON THE FUTURE...

'I reckon I'll be active for another twenty years; after that, who cares?'

to tour the airport in an army jeep for a considerable time with a smile a mile wide. And why not? When he first saw this Hurricane in 1993, it was an abandoned wreck in the Russian tundra. The millennium show attracted a record crowd – 110,000 over the three days, the first being a practice day – and what they saw in Tim was someone totally staunch, whose respect for the old fighter planes and their pilots wasn't diminished by a head injury.

By now, Tim was travelling further afield. He went to Canada in 2000 to look at a new frontier – a trophy-hunting venture that the Wallis-Bringans partnership was developing in Quebec. He loved frontiers – the newer and more daring, the better. The 300 ha hunt camp, managed by his son, Jonathan, was stocked with large elk. There was sport fishing, too.

On this Canadian trip, Prue heard of an intensive speech therapy course in Toronto. She thought Tim might benefit from it. He did – big time. Being among people he couldn't understand made him focus harder than ever on his own speech. Back in Wanaka, friends and colleagues were amazed at the improvement.

In earlier years a bung leg didn't stop Tim from following his dreams. Nor, if he could help it, would a brain injury. He lives by the message on a plaque that shouts one word, 'Persistence!' He believes that persistence and determination will overcome any shortcoming of talent or education.

For much of his life, Tim Wallis has been portrayed as a dynamic, determined, self-made Southerner who likes nothing better than to be creating new enterprises and opportunities.

But there are other, softer sides to his nature. His father taught him to be a leader. An important part of being a leader, said his dad, was never to lose

Tim salmon fishing in Canada in 2004.

touch with the people around you. If you show them you can do the hard graft, you'll get their respect. Also important was not being too greedy. Tim's success in business is based on foresight, hard work and a quality that's probably best described as 'leaving something for the next guy'.

Tim's good friends, Robert Wilson and Mark Acland, consider his personality – his ability to get on with people of different cultures, rich or poor, talented or not so bright – to be one of his best assets. He can relate to anyone, anywhere.

The creator of the 'good keen man' stereotype, writer Barry Crump, once said of Tim: 'I don't know of a single backcountry bloke who doesn't respect Tim Wallis. He's way out in front. You can't not like him… no scandals, no pretensions. I reckon we could use a few more Wallises.'

Barry Crump also summed up Tim as 'a bloke who's hard to get to know', mainly because he was forever on the move – 'always just arriving or just leaving, always busy'.

Certainly Tim had a 24/7 reputation, seemingly capable of working round the clock, seven days a week.

Tim cooking crayfish at Martins Bay.

This is what one summer's day in 1993 looked like:

- 5 am, Tim flies into Auckland from Canada and the US.
- Breakfast meeting with Maui Campervan executives in Auckland.
- Air NZ flight to Christchurch.
- Late morning, Tim flies himself to Glentanner Station near Aoraki/Mt Cook in his Cessna Centurion.
- Lunchtime: opening of new helicopter base and office at Glentanner.
- Tim flies on to Wanaka for an afternoon appointment with Korean oriental medicine dealers.
- Late afternoon, another flight to Queenstown to farewell some English Warbirds enthusiasts.
- Back in Wanaka office by 6.30 pm to unload briefcase and check on paperwork.
- Home for tea shortly.

But there were many reflective moments as well that had nothing to do with business. One year, a few days before Christmas, he asked his office manager Nola Sims if she had done any Christmas shopping yet. When Nola said she'd been too busy at the office to go to Dunedin to buy presents, Tim

A Warbird special moment: Tim's Hurricane and Spitfire flying in the skies above Wanaka.
Ian Brodie

offered to take the four Sims children, whose ages ranged from six to 12 years, to Dunedin in his helicopter. They landed at Taieri Aerodrome just out of Dunedin. He gave the four kids lunch in the big smoke, then did the rounds of the shops with them before flying them home in the afternoon.

Sometimes Tim would lend money to staff members with families who wanted to buy a house or land to build on, or acquire an expensive household item like furniture or a television.

ON FLYING...

'My favourite place to fly is around the Mount Aspiring area.'

THE WALLIS SONS

All four sons of Tim and Prue have carved out vocations for themselves that align fairly closely with their father's life-long interests. The boys were brought up to be self-sufficient, to stand on their own feet. Toby bought his dad's Hughes 500, HOT, and carried on the company name, Alpine Helicopters, at Wanaka Airport, doing charter work in hunting, fishing, heli-skiing, aerial surveying and wildlife management. Jonathan came back from Canada to become, in 2005, the manager of Minaret Station. Third son, Matthew, with a university degree in commerce, focussed on selling the hunting and fishing adventure opportunities at Minaret Station. Nick, the youngest, qualified as a helicopter engineer, and has had jobs in New Zealand and overseas.

Minaret Station manager Jonathan Wallis (far left) and his brothers: from left, Matt, Toby and Nick enjoying time together at Minaret. Neville Peat

Tim's business interests made millions of dollars (at last count, he was worth $30 million). But he has also donated a lot of money and time to worthy causes.

Ten years after the Spitfire crash he remains seriously disabled and without the authority to sign cheques and make business decisions. In legal terms, this is called being without power of attorney.

Life is certainly different today. He's not the whirlwind aviator and entrepreneur he once was, although a normal day, as before the crash, starts with a swim in his pool at home. After a healthy breakfast he goes down to the office. He gets around slowly with the aid of elbow crutches or a wheelchair, with a nurse on duty to assist him through the day. He works methodically at his desk at the office, catching up on correspondence or developing an idea. When he's tired his speech becomes more laboured. He may repeat himself. Nonetheless, his social skills are more or less intact. He shows a genuine interest in what his associates and visitors are doing and he interacts with them with characteristic courtesy and charm.

He travels a lot. In 2005 he spent three weeks in the wide open spaces of Mongolia, including the Gobi Desert,

Relaxing in tussock grassland at Minaret Station with Annabel, Jonathan and Toby.

ON HIS ACHIEVEMENTS . . .

'I've followed my dreams.'

touring with friends. He also spent time in England and Canada. He's often travelling in New Zealand, attending conferences or responding to invitations.

He was a pathfinder in a great adventure in the south of New Zealand in the 1960s, '70s and '80s, involving deer recovery in some of the wildest terrain on earth. Not many people can say they developed a weekend hobby, deer-stalking, into a career that laid the foundations for a major industry, deer farming. Add to these achievements his corporate forays into places like Siberia, Vanuatu and Canada, his contribution to modern tourism and the restoration, collection and display of vintage war-planes through Warbirds Over Wanaka.

Tim has faced many adversities – a broken back, a paralysed leg, the death of colleagues in helicopter crashes, beady-eyed bankers, Russian mafia, depression, tax reforms, type B diabetes, and now a brain injury.

He's no longer fearless in the air – jousting with rough weather or taking shortcuts. Instead, he challenges himself through his ideas and through ways of overcoming disability. He remains a heroic figure.

Self-made, self-motivated, Tim has lived by the saying, 'Just do it!' Failing that, he might say, wing it!

Tim and Prue at Benfiddich, early 2005. Tim is sitting on his ride-on mower. Neville Peat

HONOURS AND AWARDS

- Royal Aeronautical Society, New Zealand Division, Meritorious Service Award for services to deer farming and the formation of Warbirds Over Wanaka, March 2006
- Laureate, NZ Business Hall of Fame (Enterprise NZ Trust and *National Business Review*) for achievements in deer recovery and NZ tourism development, and the founding of Warbirds Over Wanaka, 2002
- Speights Southern Man, 2001
- Doctor of Commerce honoris causa, Lincoln University, 2000
- Sir Jack Newman Award (NZ Tourism Awards) for outstanding contributions to the NZ tourist industry, 1999
- Christ's College Honours Tie, 1994
- Commemorative Medal (NZ Deer Industry), jointly with Sir Peter Elworthy, for services to the deer industry, 1994
- Knight Bachelor, 1994
- Melvin Jones Fellow award (Lions Clubs International Foundation) for dedicated humanitarian services, 1994
- Otago Chamber of Commerce achievement award for outstanding contribution to the economy of Wanaka and Otago, 1992
- Wanaka Rotary Club's Paul Harris Fellowship plaque for contribution to the community, 1992
- Honorary membership of No. 453 Squadron, Royal Australian Air Force (which flew Tim's Spitfire Mk XVI FUP in operations in Europe in 1945), 1990
- New Zealand Commemorative Medal in recognition of services to New Zealand, 1990
- Aviation Industry Association of NZ Special Award for development of the NZ deer industry by the use of helicopters, for the restoration and collection of vintage war planes and the founding of Warbirds Over Wanaka, 1989
- Sir Arthur Ward award (NZ Society of Animal Production) for achievements in the deer industry, 1985
- E.A. Gibson Award for services to NZ aviation, 1980
- New Mexico Department of Game and Fish, Certificate of Appreciation for helping save New Mexico's endangered population of desert bighorn sheep, 1980
- Patron, NZ Brain Injury Association; Wanaka St John Ambulance; NZ Wildlife Research Trust; Endangered Species Trust; Upper Clutha Sports Trust; Royal Australian Air Force 485 Squadron
- Life member, NZ Deer Farmers' Association, NZ Elk and Wapiti Society (founding chairman)

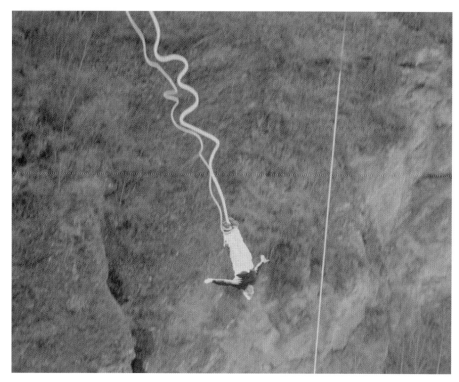

Tim's 50th birthday bungy jump. Prue Wallis

INDEX

(Numbers in *italic* indicate a photograph.)

The Brietling Fighters in a climb – from left, Spitfire, Corsair (lower), Kittyhawk and Mustang. The Breitling Fighters were a class act of formation flyers from England and New Zealand. After some 750 displays in 13 countries they disbanded in 2004. Mike Jorgensen

In memory of Ray Hanna.